Death in Poland

Death in Poland

The Fate of the Ethnic Germans in September 1939

Edwin E. Dwinger

translated by Heather Clary-Smith

8 paws an army

The Scriptorium

CONTENTS

A Word in Advance   1

Preamble   3

1 | Beginnings: September 3, 1939   5

2 | The Fate of a Bromberg Family: the Schmiedes   7

3 | The Fate of a Bromberg Family: the Radlers   13

4 | Bromberg Highlights   18

5 | The Danse Macabre Spreads   23

6 | Murder on Jesuit Lake   33

7 | The Massacre of Slonsk   39

8 | The Fate of Factory Owner Mathes and his Sons   46

9 | The Death March of Bromberg, Part 1   53

CONTENTS

10 | The Death March of Thorn, Part 1   63

11 | The Death March of Bromberg Part 2   73

12 | The Death March of Thorn, Part 2   82

13 | The Death March of Bromberg Joins With One from Pommerellen   92

14 | Towards Warsaw: The Death March of Thorn   103

15 | The Death March of Bromberg: Finally, Freedom in Lowitsch   113

16 | The Death March of Thorn: Through the Hell of Warsaw - to Freedom   123

17 | Postscript: 65 Years Later   135

18 | Appendix: Photo Documents   137

Map of the major crime scenes   154

Original: *Der Tod in Polen. Die volksdeutsche Passion,*
Eugen Diederichs Verlag, Jena, 1940.
Translation by Heather Clary-Smith, The Scriptorium.

Copyright ©2004, 2021 by The Scriptorium
wintersonnenwende.com
versandbuchhandelscriptorium.com

All rights reserved. No part of this book may be reproduced in any manner whatsoever without written permission except in the case of brief quotations embodied in critical articles and reviews.

First Printing, 2004
Second Printing, 2021

A Word in Advance

This is a translation of Edwin E. Dwinger's 1940 book *Der Tod in Polen, die volksdeutsche Passion* (Eugen Diederichs Verlag, Jena). While making this translation ready for publication we had the good fortune of coming across another book on the same subject which contained documentary photographs that fully substantiate the accounts on the pages that follow here. We hesitated for a long time before deciding to add these photos to our translation of this book because many of them are so horrible that they may shock our more sensitive readers. Still, we believe that we owe it to the brutally butchered victims from our grandfathers' generation to bring the graphic evidence of their sufferings to light. In this print edition, the photos are in a separate Appendix.

The photographs as well as their caption texts are taken from the book *The Polish Atrocities Against the German Minority in Poland. Edited and published by order of the Foreign Office and based upon documentary evidence,* published in 1940 by Volk und Reich Verlag, Berlin. In the caption texts, "RKPA." indicates findings resulting from the investigation of the Special Police Commission of the Criminal Police Office of the Reich, while "OKW. HS. In." indicates autopsy and post mortem findings. Significantly enough, this book is now banned in the vassal state that is modern Germany.

Scriptorium, in September 2004,
the 65th anniversary of the events described in this book.

This book was the hardest of all the tasks
that our age has posed me to date in my capacity as chronicler:
it contains nothing but the naked truth,
every name is that of its true bearer,
and every account is based on a sworn affidavit.

Edwin Erich Dwinger, 1940

The Protestant German Minister of the Heart of Jesus
Church in Bromberg, in silent prayer before the bodies
of murdered ethnic Germans from Bromberg.

Preamble

On November 1 of the year 82 BC, after the decisive battle of Colline Gate, Lucius Cornelius Sulla ordered the execution of those lists containing the names of all of tribune Marius's followers. With these public lists, which were called **proscriptions** even though the term had used to mean only lists with which public sales were announced, Sulla's legionaries went from house to house, killed all those who were named on the lists, raped their women to death, and set most of their houses on fire. Some 2,000 citizens were murdered that day, and **proscriptions** came to be known forever as calls to kill people who had been outlawed.

* * *

On March 30, 1282 AD, around the time of Vespers on Easter Monday, the people of Palermo rose up against the French who had unlawfully occupied Sicily under Charles of Anjou. Within only a few hours 4,000 French noblemen were killed in Palermo. Their women and children were also not spared. The raging mob dragged them from their houses and tortured them to death in the streets. Like a flame the killing spread through the entire land and marked the beginning of the reign of Peter III of Aragon. Here too, a kind of proscription list was used to identify and eliminate everyone who was pro-French. The uprising itself has gone down in history as **the Sicilian Vespers.**

* * *

On August 23, 1572 AD, Catherine de Medici, then Queen Mother of France, decided to wipe out the Huguenots. She had invited all the important Protestants to Paris to celebrate her son's wedding, and in this case the guest list doubled as the proscriptions. At midnight the alarm bells were suddenly rung, and before most of the Huguenots were fully awake they were already cut down by the henchmen's daggers. The first to fall was their brilliant leader Admiral Collignon. They were plunged out of the windows, their bodies desecrated. This murder spree claimed some 20,000 lives throughout the country and has come to be known as the **Massacre of St. Bartholomew's Night.**

* * *

On September 3, 1939 AD, the third day of the Polish Campaign, Warsaw issued a broadcast. It only stated tersely that Order 59 was to be carried out without delay. This was in fact the secret signal to execute proscriptions that had been prepared well in advance. After this broadcast the Polish people, urged on by their soldiers and officers, descended upon the ethnic Germans and murdered 60,000 of them within a few days. Only few of them were shot, most were brutally beaten to death, and even the corpses were desecrated in great numbers. **What is the name under which this deed will go down in history - what will humanity call it one day?**

1

Beginnings: September 3, 1939

In the westernmost part of Poland, September 3rd was one of those summer days one only finds in the East: the sky devoid of clouds, its blue a bit faded, and with a dry wind blowing in from Russia. In the gardens the trees were weighed down by fruit, along the fences the dahlias were bursting into bloom - if this weather held a bit longer it would make for a bountiful harvest. But would there even be time to bring it in, seeing as war with Germany had broken out two days ago?

Just as an impending thunderstorm on a hot day makes itself known in advance, a strange, gloomy tension lay in the air. For months already the Germans had suffered under Polish trespasses, but now there was something new evident in their manner: why did they suddenly look so strangely at the Germans, why did even close acquaintances no longer speak to them? It had still been possible that Sunday morning to attend church in Bromberg without coming to harm, if one avoided speaking German loudly enough to be overheard. At most one had to get out of the way of groups of singing soldiers in the streets, but most Germans did get back to their homes unmolested. And so they now sat in their Sunday best in their rooms, or if there were gardens around their suburban houses, they also sat in the small garden pavilions while the children set the tables for lunch.

Admittedly, since the first day of the war many had been arrested again, primarily of course the known leaders of the ethnic German movements, but so far no complaints about the treatment of the arrested Germans had been heard, since most of them had not returned from the prisons and one could therefore only conjecture about what was happening to them. Might the upshot of it all be a new border zone law, after the first had already expropriated so many of them? And so the German citizens continued to sit silently beside their radios and listened with pounding hearts to the German stations and to the reports of the German army's rapid advance. It's only a matter of hours, some said, before we too will be liberated here! And even if it takes a few more days, said others, all in all our time of suffering is over...

2

The Fate of a Bromberg Family: the Schmiedes

The family of the gardener Schmiede was among those waiting for lunch. Six little children run like foals around their tall mother. Finally the maid appears in the doorway, holding the longed-for bowl. They are about to sit down when the apprentice enters the room. "What news?" asks the master gardener. "Just this same call," says the apprentice, "for an hour already! Carry out No. 59, they say over and over again, carry out No. 59. I don't understand it..."

Master Schmiede bites his lips and silences his apprentice with a quick glance. But his wife has already noticed it, and asks from out of the midst of her children: "Surely they're not hatching some devilry...?"

"What should they do to us? We're all civilians! We've always done our duty, paid our taxes more conscientiously than the Poles themselves, served as good soldiers in their army... And that we don't have any weapons, well, everyone knows that too - for one thing they've searched every house ten times over, and for another, the borders have been closed for months to the point that one couldn't smuggle even a pocket knife through! It's already been a long time since they took away whatever guns were still around, and none of us could have got new ones, so what on earth could we possibly do against them? Maybe they'll drive us out of the city if they have to surrender Bromberg to the Germans, that's something we have to expect, of course..."

"Shouldn't we better flee after all?" asks Frau Schmiede in sudden fear.

"Only yesterday," says young Frau Ristau, the wife of an employee who has helped in Schmiede's nursery for years, "Pinczewski said to us, as soon as war breaks out we're going to take you Hitlers and tear you apart by the legs so that your entrails wipe up the dirt..."

"Calm yourselves!" Master Schmiede cuts them off. "Besides, it's too late, the troops are already retreating - anyone who gets between them now is in more danger than in his own house..."

He was right, it was too late. For at that same hour the Poles were already setting out on their evil deed, and suddenly thousands of them advanced through the streets of Bromberg - like a scorching flow of molten lava they filled every path and alley, penetrated every German house like in a fever. The core of these mobs were soldiers, accompanied by rabble, and students often showed them the way to their targets.

One of the first houses they reached was the Schmiede Nursery. Didn't its size and importance make it particularly hated in that part of the city? The arrivals are a group of soldiers with fixed bayonets - but what wild faces they have, are they perhaps drunk beyond all measure? Schmiede greets them with cautious politeness, but in his agitation he forgets his Polish. "You can't speak Polish, you son of a whore, but you've got weapons!" yells one of the soldiers.

"I've never had a weapon, but feel free to search the house!" Schmiede replies accommodatingly.

"What house search - three steps back!" the soldier screams in reply, lifts his gun with a jerk...

Schmiede is mortally wounded right away. His wife throws herself beside him in horror and now they fire three rounds at her, but oddly enough none of them find their mark any more. She leaps to her feet again, cries like a madwoman for her children, yanks them out the door with her and flees down into the basement with them all.

This general flight happens so suddenly that the Poles do not have the opportunity for further shooting. And so all of them reach the basement safely - six little children and their mother, her aged father, Adam by name, the nursery employee with his wife, the young apprentice, and the maid. The basement is set up as an air raid shelter, there are two water barrels there as well as several bottles full of vinegar, and a basket of towels in the corner. The escapees can only just barricade the basement door before the next shots ring out, punch through the thick boards, and shatter the window. They throw themselves on the ground for shelter, the mother lies close by the brick wall, she has pulled all her children down to her and huddles over them like a mother hen over her chicks.

For a while they lie there like that and try to calm the screaming children, while boots pound past the windows above. They appear to be looting the entire house; drapes drag past the windows next to the soldiers' boots, furniture tumbles with a crash down from the first storey, and a pile of wreckage forms in front one of the basement windows but is eventually dragged off as well. But suddenly the apprentice raises his head, his young face turns yet another shade paler, and finally he forces the words through trembling lips: "It's burning upstairs..."

Now they all hear it. It's indeed burning, the flames crackle quite audibly, the window panes above them burst explosively, and right away the draft carries the smoke downstairs. "They want to burn us all!" cries the panicked apprentice and climbs out the window in insane fear, but he has barely stood up outside before a bullet hits him in the head and slams him to the cobblestones. "Out with all of you," screech some women, "so we can do you like we did him..."

But the mother takes up the battle, the battle against the heat and the ever more choking smoke. She crawls over to the basket, takes towels out, dips them into the water barrel, pours a little vinegar on them and places one over each child's mouth and nose. Some of the children are so little that they don't understand, time and again they throw off the towels and then threaten to suffocate in an instant. With each passing minute the air grows hotter - the iron girders above them are already glowing red, and aren't some of them already sagging noticeably?

"I don't want to burn, I don't want to be buried alive!" young Frau Ristau suddenly cries, takes her husband by the hand and bolts out the basement door. Curiously they make it all the way to the street now - but there the raging mob is everywhere. The two are immediately recognized as Germans, and the civilians shout provocatively to the soldiers: "You have to shoot them down, they're real Hitlerowzi!"

Before the wife can even beg for her husband's life a bullet tears into his head from close range. A soldier throws himself over the body, pulls the new pair of shoes that Herr Ristau has only worn three times since his wedding off the corpse's feet and throws them to those who had denounced the victim as German, as a reward for their denunciation. Then he drags the wedding ring off his finger, but when the wife begs him, sobbing, to leave her the ring as a memento he beats her over the back with his rifle butt so that she collapses unconscious on her husband's body. But right away the mob yank her back to her feet by the hair, beat her to force her hands over her head, and then chase her at a run through the streets, accompanying her with shrill howls. But she is no longer the only one by any means, all the streets are scenes of such hunts, every ten steps or so there is another staggering German, most of them are covered in blood from repeated blows, some also have severe bullet wounds. Any that collapse out of weakness while running are immediately clubbed to death.

But Frau Ristau makes it - she doesn't collapse completely, she reaches the police headquarters with her last strength. An officer sits at a table. His hair is neatly parted, his fingernails are buffed, and he looks bored as he gazes at her ravaged face. "Why don't you just shoot me too," the woman cries, "I don't want to go on..."

But the officer waves dismissively, they chase her back outside, and a soldier yells after her: "A bullet is too good for you, you ugly Hitler, but no doubt someone will beat you to death!" (See Appendix, Photo Document 1.)

The young woman gets out of the building in one piece. Does she look so dreadful in her pain, with her hair falling wildly over her face, covered all over with her husband's blood, that even the most rabid of the mob shrink back from her? She washes the blood off her face in a ditch and hurries back to the Schmiede estate. Her husband's body still lies there not far from the garden gate, a howling mob dances around him, the burning house casts gruesome shadows on him, and these shadows make his shattered face seem to smile a little. "You damned Hitler are still laughing?" yells one of the soldiers mockingly, runs to a garbage can, returns with a double handful. Half a dozen rioters seize the trash from his hands and throw it at the corpse's head. But for one young marksman even that is not enough, and yelling hysterically, he stuffs the filth into the corpse's open mouth...

Even despite the hellish noise of the fire this dance of death carries all the way into the basement, where Frau Schmiede still huddles with her children. The room is gradually getting so torrid that her clothes cling to her body soaking wet, and the stone walls are so scorching hot that one can hardly still touch them. The children scream incessantly. Time and again she places fresh vinegar towels over their mouths, but she still has to do it all while crawling on her stomach, otherwise more bullets whip in through the windows again right away. Night is falling outside, and the spine-chilling howling around the house now sends almost all the children into outright convulsions. Shortly before midnight there is a deafening cracking sound above their heads, the iron girders bend almost in half, but ultimately they do hold. The house collapsed over top of them, but they were not all buried alive under it. (See Appendix, Photo Document 2.)

With the collapse of the burning house the crowd disperses, but it is not until morning that the woman dares creep out. She hopes to fetch some food for the children from some acquaintances, but only a short distance out she falls into the hands of a patrol. They immediately drag her to the police station. Only young civilians are there, and one sixteen-year-old is busy signing the death sentences. She is shoved into one of the many rooms where hundreds of Germans are already crowded together. She falls unconscious into an acquaintance's arms, but a terrible screaming wakes her again the very next moment. A Polish soldier has yelled in the door that they would all be gassed to death now. And in fact a pipe is pushed in through a window, and a strange blowing sound comes in from outside. Already they believe they smell the almond scent of mustard gas. A mindless chaos breaks out, many fall to their knees in prayer, a minister's ringing voice recites the Lord's Prayer - but none of them sink to the floor from this gas. No gas is kept in this station at all, their tormentors only wanted to revel in their agonies and have some fun with them...

3

The Fate of a Bromberg Family: the Radlers

Around the same time, they invade the home of the Radler family, whose estate is located at the lower end of the Wladyslawa Belzy. Here there are only five soldiers at first, who pretend to be looking for a machine gun. They point their bayonets at the family members, herd them from room to room, turn the entire house upside down. "Which one of you is Fritz?" one of them finally yells.

Fritz, a nineteen-year-old recent high school graduate, steps forward with calm dignity. "Where shall I stand?" he asks proudly. "You're just going to shoot me anyway." Oh, my boy, his mother thinks, I always thought highly of you, but even I never knew what a noble person you are.

"How did you guess?" the leader of the gang laughs. "Over there by the garden fence..."

Fritz wants to shake his parents' hands farewell, but the soldiers drive them all back with their bayonets. So he walks outside with a disdainful toss of his head, stands tall by the garden gate along the street. The next instant the shot already rings out, but now, when the father runs outside despite the bayonets and throws himself on the ground beside his dying son, one of the Polish officers launches himself at him in rage and hits him over the head with his riding crop. "Back into the house with you, you Hitler bandit, or I'll shoot you too!" he screams over and over again, and drives Fritz's father back inside. (See Appendix, Photo Document 3.)

Oddly enough the afternoon passes quietly, and even in the night there are no more incidents. The family sits indoors by their daughter's sick-bed. All of them think of the oldest boy. He had been an extraordinarily bright boy, hadn't he gone through his entire schooling as the best in his class? Hadn't they scrimped and saved all their life in order to be able to send the boy to college? They recall his many nature hikes, on which he had always drawn sketches since his great plan was to publish a hand-drawn travel book, a guide to their entire home region, the West Prussian region he had loved so much. The book was also to include charming little caricatures; hadn't he made them laugh many a time with his drawing talent?

"Mother," says Heinz, who is only sixteen, but with such a nobly sculpted face that he looks like a model of his race, "if the Poles should come again, I won't be able to just stand there like Fritz..." He breaks off suddenly, embarrassed, and whispers fervently to himself: "I want to live to see the new Germany, I **must** live to see the new Germany!"

At seven o'clock the next morning a cavalry unit suddenly stops outside the house, and a few riders fetch the father to water their horses at the pump. "Don't you have any milk?" one of the riders asks.

"I'll get you some," says young Heinz, runs to get a cup, and gives them milk from a pitcher.

They slurp it greedily, but one of them says: "I guess that's one of you, lying there in front of the house - served him right, the young Hitlerowzi! Now he's gaping like a fish out of water..."

"My brother was innocent," says Heinz, sobbing, "he was just brutally murdered..."

And with that, it is suddenly as though they had just waited for their cue - three at once raise their fists, rain blows on him. Heinz lifts his hands over his head, tries the get away from the blows by fleeing into the back yard garden. Two of them fire after him right away, but they do not hit him until he is in mid-jump over the last fence. Heinz gives a terrible scream - and in that scream there lies his entire youth, all his burning disbelief. He kicks out desperately, but it all does him no good, he will not live to see the new Germany...

When his father hears the shots, he wants to leave the horses at the water trough, but the soldiers point their bayonets at his chest and mock him: "It's none of your business what's going on, you just stay here and finish your job."

He continues with trembling hands to water the horses, until he hears a hand grenade explode inside the house - then he drops the water bucket and rushes into the house despite all threats. He finds the living room door shattered, but his wife and daughter are unharmed. "They hunted Heinz..." his wife can just call out to him, before they hear the soldiers roar for him in such fury that he rushes back to the pump. But this time he has barely stepped outside the door before a bullet smashes into his throat, exiting through the shoulder in such a way that it tears a large chunk of pink lung out with it.

He falls to the step outside the door, but he won't be dead for a long time yet. Foamy bubbles form at his mouth, he rolls down off the step, and suddenly cries, half-sobbing, "Shoot me dead, why don't you finish me off..." But the soldiers only laugh at his pleas, and whenever one of them is tempted to give him the mercy shot he is always stopped by one of the civilians who have been crowding into the garden for some time already. "Let him croak slowly so that he'll enjoy it," they call out to every newcomer arriving from the street. (See Appendix, Photo Document 4.)

When the mother sees her husband suffering like that, she asks her daughter to try to give her father at least a sip of water. But the soldiers knock the cup out of the girl's hand, this pretty, slender girl that looks so much like her younger brother, and kick her to drive her back into the house. "Where have you buried your valuables?" one who followed her in asks them. "Tell us this instant, or we'll butcher you!" They drag the mother across the body of her dying husband, into the garden, make her show them the spot, and quickly dig it up with their trench-digging spades.

The hiding place is only a few meters from the dying man. He constantly begs his wife for water, but again they prevent both mother and daughter from going to him. When they finally unearth the buried suitcase they howl with glee as they distribute the contents. The civilians are the greediest as they help themselves.

While they're still busy with their spoils, an officer of higher rank gallops into the yard, spurs his horse right up to the dying man, spits down onto his face several times from above, and yells down at him mockingly: "No doubt you feel better now, you Hitler bandit, why don't you scream for him..." Only after this gentleman has ridden off again, a soldier finally takes his rifle and kills Herr Radler with a shot to the head at close range, fully five hours after the first shot...

Now they drag the three corpses together, dump them outside the living room where the two women have fainted on the floor, and yell in through the window: "Now dig a hole, but make it three meters deep..."

The two women stumble outside. Their three dead are lying together in wild disarray, at the bottom is the father with his head shattered, half on top of him Heinz, with wide staring eyes, and beside them, the eldest son, his face calm and composed.

"But what shall we use to dig?" Mother cries.

"Your fingers," the soldiers laugh, "scratch like cats if you have no tools..."

The daughter fetches a rake, it's all she can find. They use it to scrape out a hollow, but how on earth should they make it nine feet deep...? The sick young girl is so weak that she can hardly stand, she helps her mother by scooping with her hands, while the soldiers revel in the sight of them: what a job for these dog-blooded Germans! But when the hole is three feet deep they are suddenly bored with it all, shove the two women back from the pit, and yell at them, satisfied: "Now throw them in, your three Hitler cadavers..." The two women are too weak, they can barely drag the lightest of the three, young Heinz, from his place. The soldiers pitch in and roll the corpses towards the hole with their feet... "And now cover them up!" their leader orders.

Frau Radler bends over the grave. The body on top happens to be her husband. "And now I should even... throw dirt on your face?" she whispers soundlessly, and suddenly shrieks like a madwoman: "No - no - no! Now it's enough, now I won't go on, just shoot me now, my daughter too..."

"Well, listen to that," the soldiers chortle, "all of a sudden! And after she's been so obedient so far! But give us twenty zloty, woman, and we'll throw the first dirt on them, and all you have to do is finish up..."

And Frau Radler drags herself into the house, to look for her last twenty zloty...

(See Appendix, Photo Document 5.)

4

Bromberg Highlights

While this went on in the Wladyslawa Belzy, another group of rabble ranged along Chaussee Street. It was led by the block commander of the Anti-Gas Protection Service, a fanatical Pole by the name of Owczarzak. Most of the group wore knuckle dusters, some carried only truncheons, others had crowbars in their hands. When they passed the house of bank procurator Finger, Owczarzak waved the mob towards the windows.

Certainly, the family Finger had barricaded the door, but the soldiers break it down with their truncheons and rush into the study where Mr. and Mrs. Finger are hiding. "Down on the floor!" one of the soldiers yells at the man. The latter lies down on the floor, his wife throws herself beside him. To the howling of the crowd the soldier presses his rifle against Mr. Finger's chest. With mechanical casualness he pulls the trigger. The sound of the shot fills the small room where one could almost expect one's eardrums to burst. Then they yank the woman back to her feet and beat her to force her to stand still. They rummage through every corner of the house and throw the valuables to the civilians. In the end they also find the couple's two young sons. To constant beatings they lead them outside, where they join up with other mobs leading entire groups to the police station.

DEATH IN POLAND

At the station the mob tries for some time to force their victims into the station with the help of beatings, but nonetheless only a few of them can still fit into the overcrowded rooms. So instead the rabble heads for the government building, but on the way there they meet up with another group, led by railroadmen from the French railway of Gdynia. "Where are you heading?" one of the civilians asks them. "We're going to hunt the Beyers!" replies one seventeen-year-old, called Gaca. Quickly the mob decides to participate in this chase, and together they march up to the Beyer property. Here too, the game begins with the same old question: Hand over the machine gun you've hidden!

The Beyer family consists of six members. Aside from the husband and wife there are two sons, one of them eighteen years old, the other only eleven, as well as an aged grandmother and an assistant named Thiede. "So you don't have a machine gun!" one of the railwaymen yells, reaches into his pocket, pulls out a cartridge. "So what's this, that I found in your study?" All of them howl with glee and Gaca demands the Beyers' immediate execution. But after a long back-and-forth they decide to take the family with them instead; that way they would have leisure to confess their dreadful crimes before being shot. "Not my little one?" Frau Beyer cries beseechingly. But they hit her across the mouth so that the blood spurts from her lips, tear the little boy out of her arms, and take him away along with the men.

As they tramp down the street again, another squabble breaks out. "The railway police should deal with them," one of the railwaymen says, "they don't belong into the government building! We want to do our share too, the city police doesn't need to get them all..." Since the rabble cannot agree, they eventually go their separate ways. While the first group returns to the government building, meeting up along the way with several other packs each leading half a dozen Germans, the group of railwaymen head for the railroad grounds. The next morning all four of their victims were found there, shot. The eleven-year-old boy was lying underneath his father; his left forearm was shattered, he had a deep cut above his left eye as well as two bullet wounds in his chest. But while the others had already been dead for three hours, this child still clung to life until noon... (See Appendix, Photo Documents 6-9.)

As the first mob approached the government building, they could already hear from a distance the sound of screaming, those chorus-like screams of people maltreated to death. Even outside the gate some two hundred corpses litter the street. As they arrive in the long corridor with their Germans, the latter see at least forty soldiers who have lined up to form a gauntlet. They are the first to have to make their way through this line-up. Blows from truncheons hail down on their backs. Several officers sit in the interrogation room; they order the Germans to kneel down and give three cheers for Marshal Rydz-Smigly. A highly pregnant woman does not understand the order right away, so a guard stabs his bayonet into her belly. When the woman's screams do not end quickly enough, the high-ranking police functionary Roberschewsk orders one of his subordinates to crank a little hand-siren to drown her out.

Owczarzak hands his prisoners over as requested, and roams through the building a little before leaving. In one room he finds ten buck-naked Germans who are being tortured to obtain some kind of confessions. Seven of them are already dead, three are still whimpering. All of them have been dreadfully beaten. At that moment Roberschewsk returns to this room, hears the whimpering, and impatiently calls out to the policemen performing the torture: "They're still alive?" He takes up the bloody axe leaning against the wall beside those who are already dead, and gives each of the remaining victims several whacks on the head...

Owczarzak returns to the corridor, where he sees with surprise that quite a number of Germans are being released. "You can go home!" the officer says with a smile. Some twenty Germans run out as though the hounds of hell were nipping at their heels. But this too is only a game. They have barely reached the gate when a dozen soldiers from the gauntlet line-up take aim and mow them down with rapid fire, shooting them in the back. So now there are not two hundred, but two hundred and twenty corpses littering the street in front of the government building.

At that moment an acquaintance who has also just brought in a group of captured Germans calls out to Owczarzak. "I know where there are some more," he calls to him, "in Thorn Street, quite a way out! But there's a woman among them, have you had one yet today...?" (See Appendix, Photo Document 10a.)

Owczarzak joins him immediately, and soon a few soldiers also fall in with them. On the way the group almost falls victim to friendly fire, because just as they are crossing the corn-market square another troop is firing a machine gun at approximately one hundred Germans who are being herded across this square to the great police prison. Owczarzak's group flees head over heels under the nearest archway and end up having to climb over dozens of corpses to get back on their intended way. Again they have to walk quite a distance, but finally they are outside the desired house. The soldiers immediately fire through one of the windows, which prompt the inhabitants to flee into a shed. They are old Mr. and Mrs. Gannot and their daughter, a girl nineteen years of age. When they refuse to come out of the shed, a soldier throws a hand grenade in. Nobody is seriously injured by it, but now the three fugitives come out, trembling. The daughter asks the mob in Polish what they had done to deserve this.

"You're Germans - and that's enough!" the civilian yells - and one of the soldiers adds: "Down with these swine!" Simultaneously he raises his rifle and hits the man in the face with the butt, and several others immediately copy him. Old man Gannot falls to the ground, and they stab him with their bayonets and fire at him six times even after he is already down. When his daughter runs for water and returns with a bowl in order to wash the blood off her father's head, they hit her in the face, left and right, and rain truncheon blows on the old mother.

Horrified, the girl flees. Skirts flapping in the wind, she runs down to the river Brahe that flows behind their estate, and in her despair leaps into the water. But the civilian cuts her off, grabs her by her loosened braid and drags her out of the water again by her hair. Some ten men now seize her at every limb and carry her into the house, into the bedroom. "Now get changed, you're totally wet!" says the civilian, strangely friendly all of a sudden. "You'll see, we Poles aren't that bad, go ahead and get changed..."

But when none of them leave the room, the girl makes no move to change her clothes and just continues to cry quietly. And at that, their patience is already at an end. Six of them hurl themselves on her, tear the clothes off her body in tatters, and throw her, completely naked, onto the floor. While almost ten men hold her down - one gags her, a couple pin her head to the floor, four hold down her arms, and two sit on her ankles - the civilian throws himself on her like an animal...

5

The Danse Macabre Spreads

The next morning, as the Polish front-line troops flood back in retreat, evidently soundly defeated in their very first encounter with the enemy and already entirely out of their officers' control, and as their escape takes them through Bromberg, the wave of destruction swells once more to gruesome heights. Is it a desire for revenge for the lost battles, for the collapse of their vastly exaggerated confidence in expectation of an easy victory - in any case it is the typical reaction of inferior characters, which by its very fact removes the Polish nation from the ranks of civilized nations: its army runs as fast as it can from an enemy whose armaments are equal to its own, but an unarmed civilian population is fair game for its unquenchable blood lust - defenseless civilians become the object of the Polish army's legendary bravery, whereas such bold daring is embarrassingly rare at the front...

The murderous frenzy escalates to heights that history has not seen since the time of Genghis Khan. All the streets of Bromberg are now a witch's cauldron, seething with pushing, shoving masses of many thousands. Anyone who falls into their hands during these hours breathes his last only after endless agonies, for now hardly anyone is still shot - almost every victim is now beaten and bludgeoned to death or ends his life under dozens of bayonets. They are nailed to the ground with bayonets, bayonets are used to dig out their eyes, old sabers serve to slice open their abdomens, and cutting off their private parts is the height of enjoyment. Outside every German house several dead lie on the pavement, the corn market square is littered with bodies, and even the last few forgotten houses are sought out now. Time and again gangs of teenaged students can be seen searching through the streets, but many businessmen also participate in the manhunt: the Polish baker denounces the German baker, the Polish shoemaker reports the German shoemaker - are these days not a god-sent opportunity for getting rid of the hated German competition once and for all? Even the educated elite participates in the turkey shoot: the Polish lawyer reveals to an eager pack where the German lawyer lives, the Polish bank director slips his German counterpart's address to another bloodthirsty mob. But at the vanguard of all these bloodhounds are the teachers, who personally lead their hordes into the German schools and act in every case as the most merciless executioners.

Is there no stopping any more in this city, is there no single pillar of humanity left? There is none, there is nothing. A minister's wife and her six children flee into the Catholic cloister - but the nursing sister, with whom she is well acquainted, won't even let her in the door: "Get out of here, be gone, there's no room here for damned Germans..." The minister's wife pleads with her, for behind her the raging mob is already closing in. But the Polish sister, the children's nurse, only yells at her more harshly and finally slams the door in her face... An old Catholic priest has only scorn for two old German men who beg him for help: "Why don't you pray to your god for help, pray to Adolf Hitler, our god means nothing to you..." No, everything is surrounded by this acid torrent, not the smallest island is left. And when anyone turns for help to his neighbor with whom he has been the best of friends for twenty years, then in most cases it is precisely this good neighbor who brings the henchmen himself just an hour later...

At long last the hordes leave the city - is the enemy so close already? Those civilians who participated in the monstrosities join up with the soldiers - do they suddenly sense the impending retribution?

Infantry Regiment No 63 from Thorn, which is still somewhat under its officers' control, moves out along the road to Hohensalza in several closed groups, but their path as well is marked by a long line of dead. In Hopfengarten, at the crossroads to Labischin, it comes across the Protestant church; the leading group immediately breaks down the church door and the first hundred flood into the silent house of God, howling wildly. They tear the church banners off the walls, fire their pistols at the crucifix, and one even climbs onto the altar to the cheers of his comrades, there to answer the call of nature. Finally they drag everything flammable onto a big pile, and from the door they throw hand grenades at it until tall flames suddenly shoot up. Within only a few minutes the old church is engulfed, a gruesome torch to light the countryside all that night long.

Moving out towards Eichdorf, the commander orders the regiment to set up a temporary position. The majority of the soldiers take cover and set up their machine guns in a westerly direction, while the rest of the gang gathers together into a small camp near Eichdorf. For the first few hours the regiment is busy, but when the enemy still doesn't arrive the majority of them again begin to roam through the countryside. Did one of them learn, by unhappy chance, that Eichdorf and its surrounding farms is a purely German settlement, created out of nothing by German farmers hundreds of years ago, inhabited by not so much as a single Pole until 1918? On the regiment's approach most of the men wisely took cover in the meadows, for by now the news of the Bloody Sunday of Bromberg has spread even to here - but the women and children calmly remained on the farms. For one thing, somebody has to stay there to look after all the livestock, and for another, surely the Poles would not attack women...

The first farm they come across is that of Lange, where they find only two old men aged sixty-five, and an eighty-year-old woman. They no longer even consider it necessary to hide behind the fig leaf that to date was used to justify each of the murders - they no longer accuse anyone of having fired on them from cover, and also no longer claim to be searching for weapons: without much ado they simply beat the three old people to the ground with their rifle butts, stab them with their bayonets, continue stabbing them...

As though this deed had inflamed their bloodlust anew, they now range from one farm to the next, yelling fanatically, and since there are some twenty-five farming estates in just a three kilometer stretch of this road and the regiment is positioned only a hundred meters west of this line, the first few shots also attract the other soldiers standing guard at their positions, so that just a few minutes later the entire host of them descends upon the three villages. In each of the houses several inhabitants are immediately beaten to death - and if the children manage to run away the laughing soldiers fire at them as they flee, "to teach them the meaning of running". Several women are felled by bayonet stabs in the abdomen before their faces are smashed to a pulp with the soldiers' rifle butts. In many cases the men are tied together with ropes and lined up, and only then are they beaten down, one after the other, preferably with blows from rifle butts to their faces. When one old farmer is unable to reply in Polish, a young officer taunts him: "For twenty years this land has been Polish now, but you, you son of a dog, still haven't learned it? But now you won't need to bother any more, it's no longer worth it for you..."

And he personally presses his revolver against the old man's eye, and pulls the trigger to the applause of the other soldiers...

On their way to the Wollschläger farm the soldiers run across the farmer Jannot's three children. The youngest is twelve, the next fifteen, the eldest has just turned eighteen years old. The soldiers stage a little interrogation, but the fact that the children do not speak Polish well quickly reveals them to be German. At that, the soldiers, laughing, stab them down despite their pleas: "That'll get rid of you, you German dog spawn..."

Farmer Renz, though he has found a safe hiding place, leaves it when he sees his two children looking for him. Little Gisela is only four years old, his son Günther has just turned nine. Out of the sole desire to take the endangered little ones into his hiding place, he softly calls their names across the meadow. The two children hurry towards him. Joyfully he takes them into his arms, snuggles them down beside him in his hollow - but already two soldiers approach, searching. They have observed the children running and followed them like dogs on a scent. They might not even have found the threesome, if the little girl had not suddenly begun to cry - and no matter how quickly the father put his hand over her mouth, the very first sound had already given the hiding place away to the searchers.

"Out with you, you damned zwab, or we'll shoot you right there in your grave!" they shout, laughing, clearly pleased with their find, and curl their fingers around the triggers.

Renz comes out, pale as a sheet, a child at each hand. "At least let these two go," he begs hoarsely, "if you won't let me..."

"That German brood? They'll go with you! Or in ten years they'll be German men, siring more German dogs, in ten years they'll be German women, giving birth to more German dogs..." Then they quarrel for a time about which of them should die first, and to top it all the most depraved of them wins, who wants to make the father suffer even the final horror. And so he finally lifts his rifle, and with one blow from the butt he smashes the four year old girl beyond recognition; the little boy, however, they have to beat to death on the father himself, who covers his son with his own body until he himself collapses from blows to the head....

* * *

But not all of them are beaten to death right where they happen to be found on the farms. One officer orders forty-six of them driven together and lined up on an incline at the edge of a little forest. "We're going to use you for target practice," he explains cynically, "that's the best way for my soldiers to learn!"

He sends a messenger to the regiment to tell the marksmen there that live targets will soon be coming over the incline and that they should practice diligently. Then he divides his victims into three groups, orders them to line up in pairs, and with an evil laugh he tells the first pair: "Now run, up that incline there - anyone who is not hit may live!"

The forty-six Germans stand as though rooted to the ground. The first two are men, one if them is Gustav Schubert, already sixty-five years old, the second is Kurt Kempf, he's only twenty-two. "You've got a chance," says the older of the two, "but my old legs..."

"What's taking so long!" the officer yells, draws his pistol. "I'll personally shoot anyone who won't run..."

And they take off - the young one in leaps and bounds, the old man can only limp. The remaining forty-four follow them with staring eyes, but even the nimble youth does not get far - there are simply too many soldiers on the hill with guns at the ready. Gunfire rattles cheerfully across the field like at a rabbit hunt. The young fellow is even the first to fall, and then the old man drops face-first...

"The next pair!" yells the officer. "Such marksmen!" The soldiers standing close-by clap their hands, and not far off someone begins to play an accordion, he plays a lively Polish folk dance.

The next pair is a married couple, old farmer Jaensch and his wife. "All right, then, Hedwig," he whispers hoarsely, "give me your hand - we went through life together, we'll go together in death as well..."

These two also do not get even halfway up the hill before they fall into the tall grass, together as they had run.

The third pair is again a married couple, Hemmerling is their name, newly wed, both of them thirty years old. At the last moment the young woman loses her nerve and it takes blows from rifle butts to drive her away from her husband. "Be sensible, Erna," begs her spouse, "you'll see, we'll make it, we're still young, we just have to run a zig-zag course..."

"Let's go, get a move-on!" the officer yells through his teeth, between which he has a cigarette.

And they run too, but the young wife is so weak in the knees that he must virtually drag her along. And so she is hit first, but from that moment on he does not run farther, he kneels on the ground beside her and takes her in his arms and rocks her back and forth, a heartrending sight, until he himself collapses silently above her...

And so it goes on, until the first group, six pairs, twelve people, are reduced to little heaps littering the hillside. Just as the officer tells the first pair from the second group to start running, a higher-ranking commander comes down the hill towards them. He gives the other only a brief glance and then says, in a voice that almost sounds choked: "That's enough murdering - the rest of you can go."

Else Kubatz, a courageous young girl standing in second position, steps forward and asks: "If you do wish to save us, please, give us some kind of paper, otherwise they'll just shoot us down in the end..."

The officer looks at her for an instant, pulls a pad of paper from his pocket and writes a few lines on it. "Now you can go home, and don't be afraid!" he says, and hands her the paper with a sketchy bow.

Someone in the group breaks into loud sobs, the girl takes the paper and takes the lead, and so the group of the saved return to their village. But they have barely reached the village street when the murderous soldier reappears, accompanied by a mob of howling accomplices. "Back with you!" he roars in a rage. "I'll teach you..."

The soldiers attack, and a few who resist are beaten to the ground. The girl offers the paper, pleading. "Give me that scrap!" yells the officer, snatches it from her hand, tears it into tiny pieces. And so they are returned to the previous place and soon are exactly where they were before. Standing in first position now is Johanna Schwarz, holding by the hand the three-year-old boy Erhard Prochnau, whose nanny she has been for years. The second pair is a young girl named Irma, and beside her the courageous Else Kubatz; the third pair are Frau Hanke and her foster son, a blond boy seven years old.

"Now move - like before!" the officer yells and draws his whip through the air.

With a sob the nanny makes the first move, but because the boy cannot keep up on his tiny legs she stops after a few steps and takes him in her arms. Johanna Schwarz has a deformed foot and can hardly run at all, only hop forward in odd kinds of leaps, and so it does not take long for one of the many bullets to find her - but she does not drop her little charge, she sinks to her knees still holding him, rolls over him protectively even in death, even though bullets also already plowed through the child's chest. A piercing scream comes from the group remaining; a young woman, bent far forward, watches the girl's course. She herself holds a six-month-old infant in one arm and a four-year-old girl by her left hand. These are little

DEATH IN POLAND

Erhard Prochnau's siblings, the woman herself is the mother of the three. (See Appendix, Photo Document 11.)

Now it's the girl Irma's turn, but at the last moment she flings herself backwards, scrambles trembling back through the line-up, and so Else Kubatz suddenly finds herself standing alone. For the time of a breath she looks questioningly at the line, but does not say a word. Just as she moves to start her course alone, Frau Hanke abruptly shoves in front of her: "Let me go first!" she gasps out. "I can't stand it any more, I won't do this any more..." She turns a little, pushes the boy ahead of herself, and says hollowly to the officer: "At least let this child live, he's an orphan, my foster son..."

"No exceptions!" he just says, "The nests have to be cleaned out too..."

The little one turns around, throws himself against her, buries his face in her apron and cries, muffled: "If they shoot you here then I don't want to live any more either..."

At that, the woman silently takes her foster son by the hand, and with a face of stone, stance erect, she silently begins to walk her path to death - the little body by her side trembles like a leaf, the little hand shivers in her large one like a bird, but not another word of complaint crosses this child's lips either. The howling soldiers fall silent for a moment - are even these monsters in human form touched by this woman's composure? Only the accordion's long-drawn tones continue, still played by the same soldier sitting on a box beside the nearby field kitchen. The fire under the cook pot crackles audibly, blue smoke curls peacefully out of the field kitchen's chimney, and only a hundred meters further on the soldiers' camp life takes its normal course as though nothing at all were happening here...

Now it's irrevocably Else Kubatz's turn. But in that instant the same commander as before comes over from the camp, stops in front of the other officer, lips pressed thin with rage, and says almost inaudibly through clenched teeth: "I already told you once that this is enough murdering!" He again takes out the pad of paper, again writes a note of free passage, again hands it to the big girl, Else...

None of the surviving thirty recall how they got away from that place of death, but all of them reached a house and none were molested further. Still that same day the soldiers dragged the bodies of the shot into Targowisko Forest, an old stand of pine trees between whose great reddish trunks many snowy birches stand in silent beauty. In the middle of this copse there is a watering hole for livestock, a deep hole in the yellow loam, into which they threw the dead bodies. But it was not deep enough to hold all of them, and so several faces remained above the water. The last to be thrown in were the little children, so that these ended up lying almost uncovered on top of the other bodies. Three-year-old Prochnau happened to come to rest beside his loyal nanny, but the seven-year-old foster son Busse lay in the arms of an old woman. As *coup de grâce* one of the Poles had brought a dead dog and thrown it in among the bodies with a wild laugh of victory: "Let them lie there together with the dead mutt, those cursed Germans, seeing as how they're dog-blooded themselves..."

(See Appendix, Photo Document 12.)

6

Murder on Jesuit Lake

At the same time another group was being herded along the road to Hohensalza, but this one passed the burning church and followed the straight road towards the Jesuitersee (Jesuit Lake).

This group included some fifty townspeople from Bromberg who seemed initially to have been taken out of the city merely to be evacuated. But shortly after they had passed the church the transport leader had them stop, and then ordered the women and children separated from the rest of the group. The women were torn from their husbands and the children out of their fathers' arms, and then the men were chased into a nearby forest clearing where they had to line up in rows of two while the women were forced to watch from their places. Two soldiers lifted a machine gun from the truck, set it up in the middle and swung it back and forth to test its mobility.

A second group of Germans arrives at that moment, but these are handcuffed together in groups of two. The machine gunners pause, and a long debate begins with the new arrivals. The German women stare numbly at the quarreling group - will their escorts get their way or will the newcomers? But in the end the new ones prevail, the machine gun is loaded back onto the truck, the new prisoners are merged into the first group, and all of them are marched off again, eastwards. Only the women and children must remain behind. They follow the procession with their eyes as long as they can but soon all that's left for them to watch is a tall dust cloud that hovers ominously over their men like a moving column.

The long line marches silently. No one is allowed to speak to another, else the guards quickly descend on them with their cudgels. Their guards are members of the military police, already infamous for their brutality. They cannot go more than ten steps without kicking someone or hitting them in the kidney area. Most of the prisoners' wrists are bloody from all this sudden yanking - since the sharp-edged handcuffs join them together without any room between, when one man is hit the other almost always suffers the blows as well. And so blood runs from almost everyone's hands, and also from many faces grown puffy and swollen from the many blows.

As they pass Jesuit Lake, which at one point comes within a hundred meters of the road, they encounter a military formation camping there. A new discussion ensues; it seems the military police do not want to go further but would rather remain in their home jurisdiction, and so they hand the prisoners over to the new military group and drive their truck back to the city. Hardly have they moved out of sight before an officer again orders the prisoners to line up in a long row, facing the lake.

There are now forty-one men in all. They stand in the white sand some ten meters from the shore. In front of them the water splashes in gentle waves, the warm wind whispers faintly through the nearby rushes, the sun glints off the wide watery expanse with summery brightness, and the sky is an unbroken holiday blue. Most of the men have come to this lake countless times to go swimming; wasn't it the most popular destination for an outing for all the townspeople? How many of their best holidays did they spend here, playing merry beach games with their wives and children from dawn to dusk! And now they are to die here, here of all places, where they spent so many happy hours?

They see before them the long boat dock, reaching some sixty meters into the water, from which they launched countless times, in groups of four in one of the light paddle boats, or even in a larger group in a sleek sailboat. They know that behind them there stand the many little pavilions where the vacationers could buy coffee, or lemonade for the children, and where bands would play in the evening to accompany carefree dancing. And now they are to die here, in their favorite place...?

They are not allowed to look around, and so the minutes turn to hours for them. They also cannot see what's going on behind them, but they certainly can hear the clanking sound of repeating rifles. It's over, they all think - farewell, you beautiful lake and blue water... Never again will I swim here, never again cross your mirror surface with light paddle strokes or glide across you with white sails... And yet not a single cry rings out, not one plea for mercy is to be heard, no matter how long the line of the doomed and no matter how many young people it includes. One of them sees his wife's reflection in the water one last time, another recalls his children playing in the sand before him, and another young fellow, strangely enough, suddenly sees again in his mind's eye a painting which he has loved for many years like no other: the execution of eleven of Schill's officers! In that painting they too stood handcuffed in groups of two, just like he and his fellow prisoners stand here today - and so he resolves to die like those officers; does he not die for Germany, just as they did? For that great Germany that he loves so ardently, for which he has worked his entire youth - now he will not see that beloved country again, now he can do only one more thing for his ancestral land, he can die an honorable death...

He has just arrived at that thought, just to die an honorable death, he keeps saying to himself, honorably like they did, like my beloved Schill officers - when a dreadful sound of firing breaks out behind his back, descends upon them from a dozen roaring guns and a hail of lead pours out at them from a dozen pistols. Half the victims collapse at once, but off to the right the boy still stands, alone, his comrade lies dead at his side, only his arm still reaches up to him, tied forever to his wrist by the handcuff. And then that young man tears open his shirt with his left hand, pounds himself on the chest with his fist, and in the pose of the famous Lieutenant von Wedell, cries until he too is mowed down by gunfire: "Heil Hitler... Heil Hitler... Heil Hitler..."

At his last cry the gunfire unexpectedly ceases. Did someone come along after all to bid the shooters stop? Did a savior turn up after all, at the last moment? Some of the dying now turn their heads, and in baffled amazement they see the soldiers flee. Most of them run in long leaps behind the pavilions, but many of them just leap in panic into the rushes. And in the sudden silence the dying men see the reason - high above them a German plane roars across the sky. The soldiers around them took cover out of fear of the German bombs.

"Can you see us up there," the prisoners' voiceless inner cry rises into the sky, "can you see what is happening to your brothers down here? Oh, drop your bombs, even if you hit us with them - give us the final triumph of letting them end in your fire..."

But a few of the victims have suddenly regained perfect clarity. In mad desperation they yank at the handcuffs that chain them inexorably to the heavy bodies of their fallen comrades. If they cannot use this moment to get away... But all in all only six men succeed in using these few seconds to flee. One of them even manages with the strength of despair to pull the handcuff off his dead comrade's wrist. The other five were unfettered, and luckily only slightly injured.

The one who freed himself of the handcuff, an older man named Reinhardt, instantly runs down to the water and swims unseen to a reed isle that hides him, and another man named Gruhl reaches one of the pavilions, among whose pile supports he vanishes. Fate catches up with the remaining four nonetheless. One of them is already so badly wounded that he dies soon afterwards in one of the boats that he just managed to reach undetected; the others are shot down like rabbits in their flight along the lake. (See Appendix, Photo Document 13.)

The German plane, however, continues on its roaring course across the sky. The pilot didn't see the massacre from his great height; and how could he guess that such things were going on! And so the Poles soon emerge again from their hiding places and descend like berserkers on the last of their victims - has the fear they just went through robbed them of their senses, has the escape of some few of their victims enraged them to the boiling point? Now some of them beat the last few dying Germans with their rifle butts, while others stab their bayonets into the falling bodies until some of them are covered in up to thirty stab wounds. Then they drag all thirty-eight people up to the dock, drag them by their arms or legs the sixty meters across the planks to the outer edge, and throw them from there into the deep lake.

But since barely half of them are dead, while most are "only" severely injured and still try to save themselves by swimming away, a renewed spate of gunfire ensues in their direction from the bridge. Some clutch the posts of the dock - blows from rifle butts smash their fingers, bayonets are stabbed into their arms - while others use the last of their strength to swim to boats nearby, where they cling to the sides with bullet-riddled hands. Their pale faces, which barely even still seem human for all the mad horror they have seen, serve as target practice until these unfortunates also let go of their last anchor and are jerked into the water by the impact.

For a long time, bloody heads still surface among the waves here and there in their battle against the water, and pleading looks are directed towards the bridge, but the soldiers' fire does not cease until even the last of them sinks helplessly into the depths...

(See Appendix, Photo Document 14.)

7

The Massacre of Slonsk

The great manhunt extends farther and ever farther. Hardly has it run its bloody course in the old German border provinces before it ranges greedily into the open countryside. Wherever there is a German settlement, even if it be deep in Polish territory, the searing sparks take hold. And so, after destroying the Bromberg region, turning the entire province of Posen to ashes and exterminating the Germans in the Thorn Basin, the flame also reaches the three hundred year old settlement in the town of Slonsk, to which a Polish king had once granted many a privilege. In this town, populated by dyed-in-the-wool Lower Saxons, there is only one single Pole among the citizenry - what could have been the reason for the persecution here? Whom had the Germans oppressed here?

A few days after the events on Jesuit Lake, the estate of Friedrich Elgert, master smith of the town of Slonsk, is visited by a cavalry sergeant and several auxiliary policemen wearing white-and-red armbands with blue imprints. Elgert and his three sons are just sitting at the table having lunch when the sergeant kicks the door open with his heavy riding boots. "What kind of gathering is this?" he barks grimly at the Germans.

"We're having lunch," the master smith says calmly.

"Do you have a radio, do you have weapons?" the sergeant asks.

"Neither," the master smith replies, and opens the adjoining door so the police may search the house.

The auxiliary policemen rummage through everything, and finally the sergeant says in German: "Tell your sons to dress warmly, I have to take them with me, they're to shoe some horses for the squadron..." And they take the three sons in their middle and lead them away in the direction of Chiechozinek.

That same evening a cavalry patrol rides into the town and searches all the houses for publications from Germany. The ulans pull out each and every drawer, scattering the contents through the rooms. The patrol leader pockets a fountain pen, while the soldiers help themselves to the silverware. A civilian auxiliary policeman who happened to have gone to school with one of the young farmers manages to tip his acquaintance off that he should flee as quickly as he possibly can, since General Bortnowski had ordered that all Germans are to be exterminated. Bortnowski is the leader of the so-called Corridor Army that is posted in the ancient German provinces. Since the young farmer takes this advice immediately, he is one of the few men to survive the massacre of Slonsk.

On the estate of farmer Koerber the same patrol demands oats, and the farmer's son must deliver sixty kilos of it to Chiechozinek. Some time later the son actually returns to the town unharmed. But that same afternoon the patrol returns and demands another sixty kilos of oats, and this time the farmer goes along with his son, urged to do so by a vague fear. After they have unloaded the oats, both the son and the cart are detained further. "You can go," the old man is told.

"But I already have two sons in the war, he's my last, how am I supposed to do the fall tilling without him?" the farmer asks.

"If you want you can stay yourself!" is the reply.

So he returns home alone, without the beautiful horses, without the cart, without his son.

The farmer Gläsmann is visited by an officer from a mounted patrol who also demands a two-horse cart full of oats. Before leaving the officer examines the farmer's papers as well as those of his son, and then returns the farmer's passport with the comment that since he had served in the Polish army he was probably innocent. "So your son will drive the oat cart!" he adds unexpectedly.

"But my son's innocent too!" the farmer cries, in dread.

"Maybe he is," the officer replies, smiling, "but he's a young German..." And so this son as well drives away, looking back for a long time.

This patrol also makes the rounds on all the five neighboring estates and fetches all the old men, marches them to the oat-laden cart of a farmer who had already given up all his horses to earlier patrols, and forces the men to pull the heavy cart four kilometers to Chiechozinek, at a run. The ulans, that respected mounted troop from Polish days of old, ride to either side of the procession, striking the men's heads with their swords so that soon all the faces are streaked with blood. Whenever any of them fall down in exhaustion - there are several eighty-year-olds among them - the ulans strike down from their horses, splitting the aged victim's skull. Only a few of them reach their destination; most of them meet their end prematurely on the dusty road...

* * *

The same day a cavalry patrol, accompanied by three civilians evidently familiar with the town, pass and then stop at the school estate belonging to the teacher Daase. Only the teacher's wife and her two adult daughters are home. The Daase estate includes a sizable house comprising not only the teacher's home but also a school. There is also a large adjoining prayer room almost resembling a small church. On the other side is the cemetery, shadowed by ancient pine trees. In the orchard, lining the street, stand sixty bee hives - are these the reason why the riders suddenly stopped here?

They come crashing into the house and ask first about the radio, second about German books and third about hidden weapons. The radio is immediately smashed with their rifle butts. Some few German books are thrown onto a pile. The search for weapons is in vain, as always. After the search the interior of the house looks like a battle field; in the bedroom the riders stomped around on the bed in their boots, while in the kitchen they threw all the food and supplies on the floor. They also helped themselves to whatever took their fancy: all the zloty they could find, a pocket knife, a lady's gold watch. (See Appendix, Photo Document 15.)

When they enter the prayer room, a touchingly plain and simple affair, the patrol leader contemptuously spits on the floor in front of the altar table. "Protestant heretics!" he says grimly. "Your husband is a minister...?"

"My husband is a teacher!" Frau Daase says quietly.

He whips around and grabs her by the arms. "Where is he?" he hisses.

"He was already taken away the second day of the war," Frau Daase replies, "to be imprisoned somewhere in the east."

"Psyakrew!" the officer curses. "That's really too bad, but they'll get him, even there they'll get him..."

The last room he searches is the school room, a bright airy room, almost charming to look at, with its little bench seats. "And he taught German - of course - in this devil's den?" he forces out through clenched teeth, and spits again, in a wide arc over the benches. "Well, that's over forever now - you won't teach another

DEATH IN POLAND

German word - in our holy Polish nation! Just a few more days and we'll be in Berlin, and then we'll dictate you our terms..." He turns on his heel and goes back into the kitchen. "And now, hand over the honey - at least sixty pounds!"

Frau Daase bows her head and fetches all the jars. Close to sixty pounds, that's all she has in the house... But she hands it over almost gladly. What does any of it mean, in light of the blessed fact that her husband isn't here, that he did not fall into their hands! And it seems that they will leave her daughters alone too, apparently these fellows are not interested in harming them...

The riders stuff the honey jars into their saddle bags and ride back up the road to Chiechozinek. As they pass the beautiful bell tower that stands on the left near the Daase estate - a marvelous old timber-frame construction dating from an earlier century which now in a sense provides the church tower to match the Daase prayer room - the patrol leader spits at it too.

Frau Daase and her daughters are almost cheerful that evening - but their relief at the harmless end to these events is premature. Shortly before midnight there is again a resounding knocking at their door, and when Frau Daase opens, the three civilians from that afternoon enter. One of them immediately leads Frau Daase into the kitchen, orders her to stand in a corner, and sits down to guard her with his bayonet at the ready. The two other civilians, of which one carries an old saber and the other a Browning, each take one of the daughters. The first takes the older sister into the bedroom, the second leads the younger into a smaller chamber.

"I have to body-search you!" says the one in the bedroom. He orders the girl to sit down on the sofa, sits down awkwardly beside her, and begins to grope her all over her body. Drool runs from the corners of his lips. The girl sits still, trembling, and begins to cry softly. Suddenly he throws her on her back and yanks her skirt off. She fights him off with all her strength and shrieks for help. For some time they fight each other, but in her desperation her strength is a match for his. Then he angrily draws his Browning and holds it to her temple: "Give it up, you dog-blood, or I'll shoot you..." But she does not give up even now, and bravely fends off each new attack. Finally he backs off and puts the revolver away. "If I shoot you, what good would you be to me then, do you think I want a corpse..." he sneers.

He goes into the smaller chamber, where he finds the second girl sobbing on the bed while the civilian is rolling himself a cigarette. "You've got to help me," he says darkly. "Seems you've had better luck than me..."

The second civilian laughs hoarsely and follows him back into the bedroom. The girl has fled into the farthest corner of the room, but now all her fighting no longer does any good. The two men leap at her and knock her to the floor - and while one of them chokes her by the throat so that she grows weak from lack of oxygen, the other furiously throws himself on her and has his way with her with inhuman brutality...

* * *

The following morning, more patrol appear. They are all coming from Chiechozinek, where a higher cavalry commando is based. Once again some farmers are conscripted, along with horses and carts. So far not a single shot has been fired in the town, and yet fewer and ever fewer men are left with each passing hour. This goes on for several more days, and finally there is hardly a man left in all of Slonsk. Where, for heaven's sake, did they all get to - are they never going to come back to their town?

No, they are not coming back, and they are never going to come back. One day, by accident, a mass grave was discovered, containing the corpses of fifty-eight men from the town of Slonsk. In this grave were found the master smith Elgert's three proud sons, with their faces so horribly mangled that their father was able to recognize them only by their clothing. One had been relieved of his new shoes, and all of them were without their warm winter coats. Young Koerber was also found in this grave; they had not let him go again. They must have shot him in the face while he was holding his hands before his eyes, for both his hands were shot through. The grave was also found to contain the young farmer Gläsmann, whom the officer had pronounced guilty for the sake of his German ethnicity, and it was also found to contain all the sons of Gläsmann's neighbors; some of them had had their bellies cut open; others were found to have been blinded, their eyes stabbed out. One man's tongue had been cut out, another's heart torn out of his chest.

And finally the grave also contained the old men who had been forced to drag the oats cart out of town. One ninety-year-old was among them, and many an octogenarian. Not one was under seventy.

So it was only as corpses that the men of Slonsk returned home - to their cemetery under the pines.

8

The Fate of Factory Owner Mathes and his Sons

Already on the day the war began, groups of people to be "evacuated" were herded together in Bromberg. Evidently they were at first supposed to be shipped off by train to be imprisoned in the East, but since the rail lines were totally jammed they were eventually marched off on foot. One of the first major groups of "evacuees" was that from Bromberg which included Dr. Kohnert, today the leader of the ethnic Germans in Poland. Another such group was "evacuated" from the Thorn region under the leadership of the Reverend Dietrich, and one of the last was the small column of some two hundred men who were assembled outside the train station barracks in Bromberg.

In the evening of Bloody Sunday the furniture manufacturer Mathes is among those being herded into the barracks. He is accompanied by his two sons, one fifteen years of age, the other only thirteen. In the middle of the riding hall they see a waist-high podium beside which stands a young officer holding a riding whip and making sure that each new arrival jumps onto this podium with a single leap. Anyone who can't do it on the first try and attempts instead to climb up is beaten mercilessly for his efforts. The hall grows more and more crowded with each passing minute; most of the arrivals are fathers with their sons, and the majority of them already have blood running down their faces, some have crushed lips, and most have had their noses broken by blows from truncheons. Finally, four hundred men are crowded together on the podium. Even though the soldiers standing guard over them behave like a horde of devils, the captured men uniformly maintain their firm and calm composure.

This composure is shaken only once, around midnight, when a young man about twenty years of age suddenly steps to the edge of the podium, raises his arm and cries down at the soldiers: "Heil Hitler!" He cannot even finish his cry, for already in the middle of the Führer's name a bullet tears into his body, and with arms outstretched he falls into the sand of the arena below. A gurney is dragged in and the man is rushed out of the arena. "We'll teach him to give your salute..." the soldiers rant, and entire groups of them follow the gurney out.

After a while, the officer calls, "Anyone who has military papers, report down here!" A number of men climb down from the podium. Their papers are simply taken from them, and they are told to pick them up again from the Commissar tomorrow. Some time later about half of them are chosen to unload ammunition from the trains in the yard. How could these men have guessed that they would get off with their lives, as almost the only ones among all those in the barracks? About two hundred men are selected for this work, the other two hundred are marched off. They are led onto Kujawier Street and herded off into the direction of Brzoza. Already outside the barracks gate a wild mob awaits them, armed with all sorts of murderous implements. Some are swinging ancient sabers, others hold daggers, many clutch wooden axes in their tense hands. These civilians lose no time beating down on the captive Germans from all sides. The guard soldiers do not try to stop them, they only see to their own protection so that none of the blows land on them - but when some of the older men cannot keep up for lack of oxygen, the soldiers themselves urge these men on with stabs from their bayonets, so that even after the first hundred meters many of them collapse, and the mob descends upon them like a black swarm of crows.

Just outside the town they are suddenly told to "Stop!", an officer gives a brief speech and closes with the order to give three cheers for holy Poland. "If you do it loudly enough, you can go home right away..."

The prisoners comply raggedly, but their cheers can barely be heard over the raging mob. Then, oddly enough, they really are permitted to go. The entire group turns back to the town. But hardly have they made it back to Kujawier Street No. 50 before suddenly gunfire rips into the group from all sides. "Didn't I know it!" cries the furniture manufacturer Mathes, covers his two sons with his body with the experience of an old front-line soldier and pulls them down onto the pavement.

After the gunfire has ceased, the survivors are again herded together and marched off in the same direction as before. Only some one hundred and fifty people are left now. Those that remained on the pavement, injured, were killed by the surging mob. For two hours the survivors are marched quickly towards Brzoza. At first everyone who cannot stand up to this forced march is shot, but soon the officer gives the order not to shoot any more because of the noise the shooting makes. And so the soldiers now use their rifle butts to beat to death anyone whose age proves to be too much for them. Time and again the prisoners hear the dull blows, which resound through the night despite the sound of the many marching feet and are usually accompanied by another sound, that of something shattering and bursting.

At Milestone 10 the vanguard turns left into the woods, and from here the column is led three kilometers to Piecky, where the remaining survivors are penned into a rickety cattle shed that threatens to collapse at any moment. It's about five o'clock in the morning and growing light enough to see again. Mathes does a head count and is horrified to find that there are only forty-four of them left now, that more than a hundred had lost their lives on that last short stretch of road. After the forced march everyone is beginning to suffer from thirst - the dusty road has parched them all. But they cannot even lie down, since there is not nearly enough room for them; and so they fall asleep still standing crowded together.

Around six o'clock a Corporal enters and asks if anyone present can speak Polish well. Little Heinz Mathes, the younger of the two sons, such a cheerful-natured lad that no-one can help but like him, immediately goes outside with the Corporal. A short interrogation ensues, during which the soldiers doggedly try to find out whether there are not some among their prisoners who had shot at Polish soldiers from ambush. The lad manages to talk them out of this notion, and cleverly hints that his father is a wealthy man who has many valuables with him. "If you take us three home alive," he finally says, "we'll give you all our money at home." They laugh at his boldness and send him back into the shed...

A quarter of an hour later they call him out again and resume their interrogation. When he returns into the shed this time, his face is pale. "I happened to hear that they've sent for gasoline, to burn us up right along with this shed!" he whispers in his father's ear. "We children are to be sent home, but that's all I could achieve..."

Another hour passes - what an hour of torment! Will they really be burned to death? Can no-one save them from this at least - do they really have to beg for a bullet to ease their end? The prisoners wilt visibly at this thought, and after learning of their intended fate many of them no longer have the strength to remain on their feet and to repress the tears.

But suddenly, at six o'clock, they are all called outside and are given a cup of coffee and a piece of rusk at a Polish field kitchen standing outside the shed. Hope rises in them: "We're going to live!" Only the lathe operator Döring says, with tears in his eyes: "But what if it's our last supper..." Young Heinz as well is hopeful again, especially since he just overheard that there was no gasoline to be found anywhere.

But poor Döring was right. The group had barely finished their coffee and returned to the shed before the soldateska suddenly surrounds the old hut and begins to yell, over and over again: "Out with you, three at a time..."

The three standing closest to the door go out. Hardly have they taken a few steps outside before there is a crack of shots. The soldiers roar: "The next three..." And another three go out. What else should they do? And they are all so tired, so inhumanly worn out, so unbearably tormented, in their spirits as well as their bodies, that most of them even long for death and see it as a blessed release...

Another three, and another three. Gradually there is more room to move in the shed, and some of the prisoners quickly drop to the ground to feel one last time the bliss of rest, no matter how brief. Finally, even though it's not his turn yet because he happened to be right at the back with his father when the execution of threesomes began, little Heinz courageously approaches the door once more, and asks the soldiers to at least spare him and his brother, as they had promised him before... Now the reply is a stab from a bayonet that pierces his tender shoulder - and at that, even this brave young boy loses his courage and he throws himself sobbing into his father's arms.

Another three, and another three. Suddenly they hear the Corporal saying cynically: "We're almost out of bullets - the last are too good for these dog-bloods - stab them with the bayonets from now on..."

And another three, and another three. But since they know about their new fate, they no longer go out so calmly - not even a bullet will release them quickly - they can no longer even hope for *that*! And now there are also no more shots to be heard, instead they hear choking cries through the wooden wall - "My God... Oh heavens... Oh Jesus!" - and then, usually, a few more muffled sounds of blows, and that bursting sound they already know so well...

Now it's Mathes' and his sons' turn. Together they are three, isn't that a great comfort in this terrible hour? Only five more stand behind them, clutching the wall like madmen. They won't be going on their own... Mathes takes his sons by their hands, walks out the door between them - the thought pounds in his head: if only I had gone right at the start, then at least my boys would have been shot, not killed in such a horrible way...

But as they step outside, no bayonets are lifted against them. The two Corporals who repeatedly interrogated Heinz rush towards them and push them a few steps away from the pile of corpses. "Now give us what the little one promised!" one of the Corporals says greedily. And so the three of them awkwardly empty their pockets, give one of their captors this and the other one that valuable piece. But they just can't please the two, each of them glances suspiciously at what the other is being given - and finally they erupt in a sudden quarrel, both reach for the golden watch being handed over, tug at it like a pair of dogs at a bone.

The old soldier Mathes seizes the moment, briefly looks each of his sons in the eyes, and with the very next breath they are running with long strides into the woods. For all their greed, the two Corporals can't even shoot at the three - by the time they have found their rifles, the refugees have already vanished among the trees...

For four days they wander through the woods without even a bite to eat or any water at all. They pick berries in the forest, lick the dew off the grass, and on the third day they catch and eat frogs so as not to collapse from hunger. But their tongues grow thicker and thicker, their lips are swollen, and on top of everything else it's bitterly cold at night and they are in shirt-sleeves. At night they sleep in thickets, making nests for themselves like deer, but in time their feet also split, since their shoes were already lost on the first march. Little Heinz holds out most valiantly here as well, even though his pierced shoulder hurts and a strip of his father's shirt is his only bandage. During the night from Wednesday to Thursday no dew forms, and despite everything they now feel their end is near. Also, they have gradually drifted into the war zone, scattered soldiers roam the woods everywhere and the fear of being captured again drains their strength. When brother Horst collapses for what is evidently the last time, little Heinz pulls a piece of bread from his pocket and holds it out to him mischievously: "I've been saving this until now - see, we're going to live at least another few hours!" he says triumphantly. Isn't he a real hero, this young German boy - secretly saving an iron ration, not touching it for four full days! And despite being only thirteen years old, he was right - this piece of bread brings even Horst back to his feet once more, and with renewed strength they walk on, farther westward...

At two o'clock in the afternoon, after a four-day march, almost without anything at all to eat, and no water except dew, they reach the German troops - the only three survivors of that death march that numbered two hundred people as it left Bromberg but which is known as the Death March of Piecky, for the place where it ended.

9

The Death March of Bromberg, Part 1

At the time this death march left for Piecky, the one that included Dr. Kohnert had already been on the road for two days. This group had been assembled in the Reich War Orphanage, a multi-story building with many large rooms and a long garden that stretched behind the house. Already on the first day of the war its rooms had begun to fill with prisoners, but at that time the arrests were still being carried out in a normal manner; the general psychosis did not descend upon the country until September 3.

In those early days the arrests generally took the form of a police officer entering the "suspect"'s home, searching it, confiscating all radios and finally demanding the home owner's signature on a piece of paper to confirm that the house search had failed to turn up anything of interest. In most cases this ticket doubled as the arrest order. Some Germans were instructed to keep it as ID, but usually they were arrested on the spot. Three kinds of tickets were issued during this wave of arrests: the first were red and were given to those to be arrested, the second were pink and were issued to those to be interned, and the third were white and went to those to be evacuated - but nonetheless all three kinds of prisoners were treated exactly the same. Later it turned out that the recipients of the red tickets were the most hated, and accordingly, they were the most likely of all to be shot.

In the evening of the first day of war, then, the orphanage is already half full, and new prisoners are brought in all night long. Many of these early arrivals were able to bring some luggage: well-packed backpacks, baskets with food, items that revealed at first glance that they had been readied long ago on the basis of some sort of premonition. But only the first were arrested in this orderly manner; the later the hour, the less prepared the new arrivals were. Many of the last of them did not even have a coat, they came shuffling along in their slippers. However, the streets themselves were still calm at this time. Since all contact with the prisoners was prevented once they had been arrested, the Germans themselves had no idea of the scope of the arrests and anyone who had not yet been personally affected continued on in blissful ignorance.

On September 2 Dr. Kohnert, the well-known leader of the German Organization, is brought in. He is a slim, strikingly tall man whose long face and light eyes hint at unusual energy and an ironic wit. He is silently directed to assume leadership of the prisoners, and from the very first day he devotes himself selflessly to their benefit, an undertaking that soon becomes an ever greater risk to his own life. That same day, Adelt arrives, and with him the young Baron von Gersdorff, both of them leading men in the ethnic German movement. More and more acquaintances meet up in the orphanage rooms, and it soon becomes clear that those ethnic Germans who had been politically active had been arrested first.

The first bombing attacks are flown on Bromberg on Saturday around noon, and the crash of the detonations pierce even the pandemonium of the overcrowded rooms. Everyone rushes to the windows, hoping to see one of these nearby explosions or maybe even a German flier himself. But instead of German pilots they only see

DEATH IN POLAND

German peasants who are just then being herded past the orphanage. For the first time they see that these peasants are being herded along to brutal blows with truncheons. A few women cry out in horror, one of them collapses in an epileptic fit and continues to shriek while lying on the floor. Instantly the guard soldiers' brains short-circuit, and they force themselves into the rooms from every side with their bayonets fixed and force everyone to drop to the floor where they stand. "Anyone who gets up will be shot!" one of the officers screams. And so they lie on the floor, almost on top of one another, stare aghast into their guards' faces, almost unrecognizable with agitation, and at that moment they sense for the first time what kind of storm clouds are gathering inescapably on the dark horizon of their future.

At five o'clock in the afternoon everyone is herded outside and made to line up in rows of twos in the backyard garden. A few soldiers from Haller's Army approach, select some prisoners simply on the basis of their looks, and handcuff them together in pairs. With clever insight they have managed to identify almost all the leaders. Then an officer arrives on the scene, orders everyone to form a square, has his men load their carbines in plain view, and then calls in a hoarse voice that anyone attempting to flee would be shot at once. Then the crowd marches out in rows of four; the first column to move out are the men, then the women follow. All in all there are eight hundred people from all walks of life: lawyers walk beside laborers, servants beside secretaries. All ages are represented as well. There are old men, and some women carry babies.

There are some two hundred guards, one per line of four prisoners. The majority of them are the so-called *strelzi* (marksmen), a kind of paramilitary youth group to which almost the entire active Polish youth belongs. They had already been running around armed for three months or so, but acted more like louts than like a real danger.

The rest of the guards are from the regular police force, to whom some auxiliary policemen have been assigned. These are dressed in ragged civilian clothing and are recognizable only by their red-and-white arm bands. The Commandant of this marching column is the last Police Commandant of Bromberg, an older officer with an evil reputation, but at first he still shows some common sense and decency.

The first stop is at the police administration building, located beside the police prison. In the back yard of this building everyone is allowed to sit or lie down for a bit. It will be the last rest before a long march. A step-like wall separates the prison from this yard, and the gloomy impression of the barred windows descends like a weight on their souls. No doubt they too will be behind such bars soon - and many of the men who had been in leading positions in the ethnic German community already know from bitter experience what it really means to be incarcerated in a Polish prison. And so most of the prisoners sit silently beside each other, the women on the right, the men on the left. Among those that do speak, the conversation is mostly about the arrest papers. They show each other their tickets and try to guess what the colors mean. One man who speaks Polish well translates one after another, and as it turns out, the red ones are doubtless the most dangerous to have, the pink were issued primarily to the Reich Germans, and the white ones to people in the Poles' good graces.

"I'm just going to throw my red one away," says one young man. "Better not to have any, than this dangerous document."

"It may be better, or it may not!" says another. "Maybe it's worst not to have a ticket at all."

"Or maybe it's best..." the other retorts.

"Besides, it's obvious that the lists that were used as the basis for the arrests were already drawn up months ago!" Adelt interjects.

"Many women who are now married were arrested under their maiden names, and in some houses the Poles even tried to bestow such tickets on deceased people."

"They must have been drawn up in late April," adds Dr. Kohnert, "because nobody who moved into the area later than that has been arrested."

"Also, some people who moved to other houses were still being sought in their old homes!" Adelt speaks up again. "So that's a definite proof that all this was planned a long time ago. And besides, unlike everything else, these raids are so well organized that the Poles could not possibly have done it all by themselves. Sympathetic organizers from abroad must have helped them!"

"It's said that in the cities in the northwest there were even trains at the ready," Dr. Kohnert says, "and it was only the rapid advance of our troops that ruined those plans. But now they say, better that the prisoners should all die than that the Germans should liberate them..."

"Do you think they'll catch up to us, our brothers, the German soldiers?" someone asks quietly.

"I'm sure of it!" another whispers.

"It depends on how quickly they herd us along," Dr. Kohnert speaks up again.

"But the women... it's not possible..." another one whispers, appalled.

"Everything's possible - at least in Poland..." says Dr. Kohnert harshly.

Gradually night has fallen, and at last it is time to move on. As they exit the garden for the street, they see that there is already a wild mob awaiting them there. They have formed a sort of double-walled passageway for them to run the gauntlet through, and beat down on them with all sorts of objects. The brutish expressions on their faces are so alien that it is doubtful any of their victims would ever recognize them again. Only a few recognize a Polish physician, he is a well-known doctor in town, an acknowledged, intelligent man - what has gotten into him all of a sudden? He is literally foaming at the mouth, beating at the prisoners with both fists, behaving truly like a madman. The prisoners at the vanguard have the worst of it, they must literally break through these human walls, but fortunately almost all of them are younger people, mostly the tough leaders of the ethnic German community, they lift their arms protectively over their heads, duck and force their way through. The crowd hurls rocks, flings filth from the street at them and accompanies it all with a chorus of abuse whose main theme is the most vile and repulsive Polish curses.

The women are no better off, for here it is the Polish women who see that their hour has finally come. They grab for the German women's hair with hands like claws, tear down their braids, and clutch and hang on so fiercely that many of them are dragged along for several meters. Many of the prisoners have scratched faces after only a few steps. A few of the Polish women have even brought along some old-fashioned hat pins and coldly, deliberately stab at the Germans' eyes with them. When one woman carrying a baby comes out onto the road - the crowd of fellow prisoners have already taken her into their midst, knowing that they would have to protect her - a particularly vicious shrew throws herself furiously on the child and tries, screeching, to tear it from its mother's arms. After only a few meters all the women walking on the outsides of the rows of prisoners look as though they had been roaming the streets for months: the hems of their skirts are trodden down, large tears disfigure the thin blouses, some are missing an entire sleeve or both. Aside from all this, the prisoners are also pelted with all the dirt and filth that the mob can scrounge out of the gutters in their hurry, and all the curses that make up the choice vocabulary of the Bromberg prostitutes are spewed after them to hurry their passing...

Finally things look up a bit. The column has reached the city suburbs. But here too there is still a shoving and seething crowd, as transports arrive simultaneously in almost all the streets: some are arriving from the region of Thorn, others from the area east of Deutsch-Krone where the German army had already broken through, and still others arrive from Hohensalza. It is a terrible confusion, drowned out by the never-ending yelling of the guards. Almost all intersections are jammed; every Commandant tries to move his group through the others, and often this results in vicious clashes between the guards themselves. After that, they march for half an hour, almost unmolested except for the constant prodding by the *strelzi*. They all heave a sigh of relief. The fresh night air is soothing - but this bliss doesn't last long. Another mob awaits them at the brickworks. They are the brickworkers, the most disreputable folk in town. They have even brought the tools of their trade with them and are standing at the ready with crowbars in their hands, others with long wooden paddles. Once again a hail of blows rains down on the prisoners, and the first of the old men collapse under it. They are left to the mercy of the brickworkers - for once anyone has collapsed on the ground, not even the best of comrades can help them, they would only be beaten down themselves for trying to give aid...

They pass the huge lumber wharf. The water gurgles to them softly, and some of them are already tormented by thirst but anyone who takes even a single step out of line is immediately beaten back by the *strelzi* with their truncheons. A fortune in rafted lumber floats off the wharf - they won't be able to help themselves to that any more, some of the Germans think, as though in a sort of inner consolation.

At that time, all the farm estates in the town of Langenau were still standing, but all the doors and gates are barricaded, lights are nowhere to be seen, and neither are there any faces in the windows. There are many German farmers in this town - have they already divined what is in store for them in just a few hours? Three days later, after the army has retreated, no house is left standing here, all the farms are burned to the ground, most of their inhabitants beaten to death. (See Appendix, Photo Documents 10b and 16.) This town of Langenau is also where the first woman from Dr. Kohnert's column dies; it is seventy-six year old Fräulein Schnee, a niece of the well-known Governor of German East Africa. She has devoted her entire life to the service of the poor and had been in charge of the public welfare organization of the ethnic German community in Poland. Now, in her dying moments here, she had to be left to the merciless hands of the mob. With snow-white hair, eyes wide, her entire wrinkled face an unearthly shade of yellow, she lies there....

The huge column marches on, passes through Schulitz, where once again a mob awaits them. Beyond Schulitz things finally calm down somewhat. The population of the open countryside has been much less infected by the general incitement than the city folk, and here the hatred of the farmers generally does not exceed vulgar curses. Every now and then the men light a cigarette - as yet they are still rich, they still have a few, but only one may be smoked at a time in each row of four. After a few drags each passes it on to the next, and there is no-one who takes even one puff more than his neighbors. And so the glowing red dots move back and forth through the night and their incessant movement gives a strange impression indeed.

When dawn finally breaks and the wide-open countryside grows lighter, they witness their first air raid. The singing drone of a heavy bomber approaches above them. Instantly a mindless panic breaks out among the guards. "Into the ditches," they scream with huge anxiety, "into the ditches, right away!" They draw their pistols and raise their rifles, and the prisoners dash apart and throw themselves into the ditches to either side of the road.

"Are they doing that for our sake?" one of them asks, baffled.

"Of course not!" Dr. Kohnert says, amused. "Only to protect their own precious lives, and for no other reason than that! After all, the fliers might take our columns for troop transports and drop their bombs on us as the ideal target - and while that would only please the Poles where we are concerned, it would cost them their own lives as well! That's also the reason why we've been moving only at night, and will most likely keep moving only at night..."

"And during the days?" somebody asks.

"They will pen us into a barn or shed, a thousand in a room just big enough for a hundred!" Adelt says bitterly.

"At least that way we will actually get some rest..." says a seventy-year-old clergyman.

They fall silent and stare up at the plane, where they can clearly see the white cross on black, and also the swastika flag on the rudder. And up there sit three or maybe even five German soldiers, they think with an odd painful longing - and none of them can know that down here there are a thousand Germans lying in the ditch, and at the same time tens of thousands more throughout the country, looking up at them, hearts pounding, until their eyes water from the strained gaze...

"I've heard the Poles are already marching on Berlin!" says one young man softly.

"Right... if that were so, our fliers would definitely be here, of all places!" Dr. Kohnert replies with a laugh. "Then they would have other things to do than to fly one raid after another on Poland."

These logical words do everyone good and reassure even the most despondent. For a while longer they are allowed to remain in the ditch - what a relief for their tired legs - but in the end the plane disappears over the horizon. And soon the guards jump up again and scream at their prisoners to do the same. To the crack of blows the rows re-form, and slowly the endless column begins to move again. Once again dust rises in dense clouds from the road, settles like thick powder on every face, insinuates itself in a thin abrasive layer between clothes and skin and like fine slivers of glass into the shoes. Already that first morning everyone's eyes are red, many have sores on their bodies, and most feet are blistered.

Except for these air raids there is no rest for them. They must march fifty-eight kilometers in one stretch, for fifty-eight kilometers is the distance from Bromberg to Thorn, which the Commandant has evidently chosen as their destination. Already it is almost noon. The sun burns hot this day, thirst grows into severe torment, and ever more prisoners peer over the heads of those marching before them in order to at least catch a glimpse of the towers of Thorn. With relief lasting the space of a few breaths they see the silhouette of the old fortress, straighten their tired backs once more and forget the pain of their sore feet. Granted, another angry mob awaits them in the streets of Thorn, but by now they're used to that, it no longer intimidates them, and pressing closely together they run this gauntlet as well. Finally the hall of a suburban establishment takes them in, and in entire rows they collapse gratefully onto the bare floor.

10

The Death March of Thorn, Part 1

Aside from this great deportation death march there were countless smaller ones, trudging along almost every road through Polish territory. Who could ever name them all, locate all the graves, tell of all the horrors their victims endured? One such death march was that from the Schrodau region, and it alone left a hundred and nine victims murdered in Turek. Another was that from the Siedlce prison to the citadel in Brest, and it left twenty-five of its members dead and dying in the ditches. A third led to the concentration camp Bereza-Kartuska, and for all its members it was a march straight to hell. Of all these countless marching columns, one of particular significance, besides Dr. Kohnert's, was the column that endured the longest march of all, namely the one coming from the Thorn region, which included among its number the well-known ethnic German leader Lengner, and with him, the equally prominent Kittler and the well-known minister from Gursk, Dietrich.

This group was assembled in the police prison of Thorn after its members had first spent two days in the prison cells there. One of the first men to be brought in was Dr. Konrad Raapke, a factory owner from Thorn. He spends his first day alone in his cell, which incidentally is only meant for one inmate anyway, but on September 2 another seven men are crowded in with him. As it turns out, most of them are good friends of his, including Lengner, the leader of the German Association of Thorn, a short but physically very fit man in his fifties, with unusually bright eyes beneath a strikingly broad forehead. Later they are joined by Kittler, the leader of the Young German Party of Thorn. Thanks to the aid of a boilerman they manage to get in touch with their families, so that these can bring them the barest necessities before they are marched out, most importantly a backpack, readied some time ago in case of such an emergency.

On that infamous Sunday, which is sunny and hot in and of itself, their Polish captors turn the central heating system on full, and the afternoon becomes unbearably hot in the overcrowded cells. Since the eight men can barely even move in this cell meant for one, the heat is triple the torment for them, and soon their sweat runs in rivulets and their clothes stick to their bodies like wet rags. "That's typically Polish," says Dr. Raapke, with resignation. "But this time nobody can excuse it as 'an impulsive act by a hotheaded people', this time it's a deliberate, calculated dirty trick!"

Due to the heat, the air, which is used up anyway, becomes so unbearable that some prisoners begin to suffocate from the lack of oxygen. Everyone has to fight for air with every breath. Add to that the fact that the entire cell is covered in weeks-old grime, that hordes of vermin crawl the walls, and that shrieks of pain frequently resound from the other cells. Whenever new prisoners are brought in the cries of the maltreated rise to a gruesome chorus, clearly showing the other prisoners that the great Polish manhunt is taking on more and more horrible forms with each passing hour.

"Just think of what awaits us when we get out..." one of them whispers, shaking his head helplessly.

"It's odd," says Raapke, "I was still treated fairly decently when they brought me here two days ago. But since then their psychosis of hatred has taken on forms that one can really only describe as pathological."

Around ten o'clock at night, as their exhaustion is beginning to turn deadly, everyone is suddenly chased outside at breakneck speed. In sweat-soaked clothes they now stand in the frigid autumn night until everyone is horribly cold and their weakened bodies shiver like leaves. Then everyone is first relieved of all metal objects, such as pocket knives, aluminum soap capsules, cigarette lighters, even keys on their key chains. Gradually the guards also arrive. They consist of two units of *junaki*, a kind of organization similar to the *strelzi*, and the two hundred of them are led by an army Captain and several NCOs assigned to him. Just before the march-out several policemen also join the guards, so that in the end the escorts number two hundred and fifty, almost half as many as the prisoners themselves, of whom there are about six hundred. Among these prisoners there are numerous octogenarians, as well as about sixty women, one of whom has her child with her, a little girl just four years old.

Fifty men make up the vanguard, and then comes the marching column itself. To either side of the prisoners walk two rows of *junaki*, all of them armed with French rifles, with sharp three-edged bayonets fixed. The rear is brought up by fifty soldiers. Most of the prisoners can hardly wait until the column will finally move out, as they hope that walking will warm their shivering bodies somewhat. As the column marches off in the direction of the main train station, a few naive ones among them already expect to be entrained, but the march goes past the station and in the direction of Alexandrowo. For as long as they are still in the city streets, these prisoners as well must pass through a line-up of malicious rabble, and a few of those weakened by the heat already fall victim to their maltreatment. Speaking is strictly forbidden, as is looking around; both offenses are immediately punished by blows from truncheons. Whoever falls down with exhaustion is instantly beyond help, for giving assistance of any kind is also strictly forbidden.

Outside the city limits things improve considerably for the column of prisoners, but then the *junaki* begin to torment them. Especially the elderly are shoved forward time and again, and also anyone who is ill. There truly does not seem to be a heart beating in these young people's chests. And don't these unhappy people, with their bruised and beaten faces, look as though every raised hand should drop again at the very sight of them? A seventeen-year-old *junak* wearing the blue coverall of an apprentice mechanic has chosen a half-unconscious old woman to pick on; for the last ten kilometers he has not left her side, herds her along in front of him the entire time even though she is almost collapsing from exhaustion, and gives her countless little pokes with his bayonet. And the German men must see and watch this, watch it the entire time - and can not even raise a hand in the old lady's defense because any such movement would be tantamount to suicide. At times like this, when men are powerless, oh why do not the heavens open with a crash of thunder, to strike down such violators of nature with a bolt of divine lightning? For this here went against Nature herself, and she herself should rise up against it!

The column marches all night long, arriving in Alexandrowo the next morning. In the city, black seething masses of rabble await them once again and beat them with all kinds of objects. Near the train station, quite a distance from the city, there stands a huge customs warehouse that was once used as tobacco storage hall; the prisoners are penned into it. The great wooden hall contains no straw, and so everyone drops onto the bare floor where they are allowed to rest until the evening. A couple of times, air raids on the nearby train station take place; the pressure of the bursting bombs can be felt all the way into the hall, and the crash of the explosions rings in everyone's ears for a long time. Once more the ethnic German leaders show their exemplary characters: the rations which some few still possess are distributed fairly and equally among all. In the course of the day the leaders even manage to convince the Captain to procure some carts for the sick.

At dusk the order is given to line up, and the prisoners arrange themselves in rows of four in the hall itself. But while they are still waiting to march out, an old man suddenly moans that he would not be able to walk any more. This message is immediately passed to Lengner, standing at the front, who in turn whispers back via Kittler to Dr. Bräunert that the old man should join the other sick prisoners on the cart. At that moment a man leaps out of the prisoners' ranks nearby and demands to speak to the Polish Captain, announcing that he has just overheard a dangerous conspiracy. Evidently he is one of those Poles who had been placed in each column as spies. The Captain arrives, and listens with a scowl. "Who was whispering?" he then asks.

The spy pushes his way through the ranks and first points out Lengner, then Kittler, then Bräunert, and last at a fourth man named Oliva.

"So you planned an escape, did you - were hoping to take off, all of you!" the Captain says cynically.

Lengner tells him truthfully what they had spoken about, and says that they had whispered only because speaking in and of itself was forbidden.

"If it's forbidden, then why do you do it?" yells the Commandant.

"It's a matter of someone who is deathly ill, Captain!" says Kittler calmly. He is only thirty-four years old, a strikingly tall man, his face has pronounced cheekbones and an expression of great intelligence.

"You just see to yourselves, you'll soon be deathly ill too!" the Commandant growls scornfully. Then he turns around and yells, almost falling over himself with excitement: "Out with these four dog-blooded Hitlerowkis!"

A dozen *junaki* surround them and force them out with blows. As he leaves, Lengner greets his faithful followers and Kittler looks his friends in the eyes one last time - an offense which the *junaki* immediately punish by descending on the prisoners and pistol-whipping them in the face with their Brownings. The last thing the prisoners see of their leaders are faces quickly turning red with blood - but their heads remain proudly thrown back and they do not bow even under these blows...

Right after these four are led off, the column is marched out and forced at a run up an incline, where mounted police await them. But during this run, some few of them do manage to cast a glance backwards, and they see their four leaders standing with hands raised in front of the warehouse wall; a few also hear one of the policemen rant furiously at one of the four that he should damn well raise his hands too. And they also hear the reply, the devastating reply: "How am I to raise my hands now that you've smashed my joints..."

That is the last anyone knows of the four ethnic German leaders. Since no shots were fired, they must have been killed with bayonets. And so the sad procession moves on in deep silence, deprived of its leaders and the encouragement they had known so well how to give. Their place is now taken by Reverend Dietrich who, like them, devotes himself to his task with a degree of self-denial that soon earns him the admiration of all his fellow sufferers. The column is now almost entirely mixed, a few rows of men are followed by women, but this only puts them at the disadvantage of being treated just as cruelly as the men, which had not been the case when they were segregated.

After an hour's march, shots are suddenly fired in the vanguard - have they encountered German troops after all? For the first moment the entire escort seems to think so, and a panicked fury breaks out among them like a kind of insanity. "Hands up, you swine!" they scream. "Down on the ground, you whore-sons!" roar others. "We'll liberate you, all right - you're all going to be shot now!" shriek the remainder.

The entire column immediately drops to the ground, but even that does not suffice to calm the guards. They aim their guns accurately at the dark masses on the ground, and fire rapidly into them for several minutes. Terrible screams rise from the prostrate prisoners, many are mortally hit, others thrash about with dreadful injuries. "Whoever can still raise his head, do so immediately!" a shrill voice cries, and repeats the order a dozen times or so. A few of the women comply automatically, and another round of shots rings out and hurls them back down into the dust...

Finally the shooting ceases, and the vanguard grows quiet as well. It was no Germans, it was just a sudden panicked short-circuit. "Up!" the order goes now. "Close up the ranks!" Anyone who can still get up struggles to his feet, some of them stand in pools of blood from shot prisoners, others can only get to their knees. One young woman also tries to stand up but collapses again immediately - a bullet has smashed her ankle. "Oh, just shoot me dead..." she finally cries.

"Shut up, you whore!" roars one of the *junak*.

"Just shoot me dead, please, please, please, just shoot me dead!" she begs anew.

"Let her have it, if she wants!" yells another *junak*.

"I don't shoot at women!" says the first, with a proud gesture. Oh, after all, he's a Pole, always chivalrous to the ladies...

"Well, you sure are stupid," says the other coldly. "Aren't they Hitlerowkis too?" And he walks eagerly to her, presses his rifle against her left breast, and with a scornful laugh pulls the trigger...

Gradually the rows form again. The still-living step over the dead, walk around the dying. In almost every row someone is missing. Once again new people join up to fill in the rows, and now even individual women walk in some of the men's rows. Despite this terrible "rest period" the survivors hold up as well as before, only now and then there is the sound of quiet sobbing...

Hardly has the rear of the column left the last victims on the ground behind it before a horrible spree of murder begins - every single body on the ground is carefully listened to, and if there are any sounds of breathing he or she is dispatched for good with dozens of stabs from bayonets. For a long time the prisoners walking at the end of the column still hear death screams behind them, and the quiet calm of merciful night descends only slowly over this site of horrors...

But the march itself is growing harder and harder. Did the scent of blood whip the *junaki* into such a frenzy that they are now dreaming up ever new torments? After a short time one gives the order that all luggage is to be thrown away, into the ditches - mind you, without the slightest pause. Since nobody has the chance to take anything out first, this means the loss of everyone's last few treasures, the last rock-hard crusts of bread, the last carefully hoarded cigarettes.

"The purses too, you damned whores!" the *junaki* yell at the women. At that, Reverend Dietrich turns to the Commandant and points out to him how senseless this demand is, and actually manages to have the order rescinded. With a poke of his bayonet one of the *junaki* has just forced a young lady to throw her purse away; but hardly has this lady heard the order being withdrawn that she walks back to her tormentor, head raised high, and tells him coldly: "Pick up my purse!"

"Are you crazy?" The *junak* freezes.

"I said, pick up my purse, didn't you understand me? Don't you know what's proper around a lady?" she repeats icily.

For a while the boy stares dumbfounded into her eyes, then he surrenders to the bright girlish gaze and bends down meekly to pick up her purse.

"That's Poland!" thinks Dr. Raapke, who is standing nearby. "What a country - what a people..."

After a period of uneventful marching, another order is given: Everyone is to close up ranks tightly! At the same time the rear of the column is prodded to speed up so much that everyone ends up constantly stepping on the heels of those in front of them. Many come away from this with deep wounds in their heels, and many soon lose both their shoes. "Maybe they only dreamed this up so that the rearguard can collect all the shoes, just like that was the reason for making us throw away our luggage. There's nothing one can put past these louts, not even something that seems absurd to normal people!" thinks Dr. Raapke.

He is walking in a row of four brawny men. The row in front of him, however, is made up of four young girls who have linked arms in order to support each other better. But since the men's row is much wider than the row of girls, this is a constant annoyance to the side guards. "Line up with the person in front!" one group yells constantly, and shoves the men with their truncheons from the right. "Walk in exact single file!" yells the other group just as constantly, and shoves them in the same manner from the left. Finally the young girls realize that they can only keep the men behind them from suffering constant blows by unlinking their arms again and walking at the same distance and in a row of the same width. Walking among these girls is a certain Fräulein Buller, a secretary from the German Consulate, a remarkably delicate girl but she holds her own in exemplary fashion.

Hardly have the prisoners adjusted to this harassment before the *junaki* think of something new, and yell as in a chorus: "Dropping to the ground doesn't go smoothly enough yet, do you think we're going to risk bombs hitting us for your sake? So let's practice, down on the ground, all of you as one, when we give the order..." And then each of these boys yells whenever he feels like it: "Down..." So there are always a few rows of prisoners down on the ground. If they do not comply quickly enough they have to repeat it a dozen times - but if they do comply with precise suddenness and to the guards' satisfaction, the row behind them usually falls over them due to the unexpected stop.

"Hahahaha!" the *junaki* then laugh, slap their thighs, roar at the top of their lungs: "See them tumble, those elegant Hitlerowkis, falling over each other like rabbits..."

The last torment of this stage of the journey comes in the form of an order for everyone to walk with their hands behind their backs. And so they march the last few kilometers with their backs ramrod-straight, which quickly becomes so painful that not only the women moan softly with every step. Having to walk like this robs one old man of the last of his strength, and in a fit of weakness he staggers in front of an oncoming truck, which crunches right over his body...

In the gray of dawn they finally see a large estate, which is already full of soldiers but which also has a number of barns beside the stables. This is the Jarantonice Estate, the second day's intended destination - but when Reverend Dietrich does a head-count, there are fifty fewer than there were the evening before.

11

The Death March of Bromberg
Part 2

Contrary to expectations the column of Bromberg deportees also stayed in Thorn for the night. The forced march of fifty-eight kilometers seems to have exhausted the guard troops to the point where even the bad news arriving from the front fails to make them eager to move on quickly. The leaders of this group try without success to obtain some food from the city for their people. After they have finally found a seemingly humane guard who, after much persuasion, accepted their collection of one hundred zloty and agreed to buy some bread for them in the city, they waited in vain until nightfall for him to return. But finally they realized with a sinking feeling that this lousy fellow had cheated them out of their last bit of money. And even water was withheld from them, no matter how much and how often they begged for some, so now they have gone without anything to drink for thirty-six hours.

If at least they were completely amongst themselves - but they too have been seeded with Poles from the start. Some of these are simply criminal convicts, but others are spies deliberately chosen for this purpose, and many of them speak German without an accent. In the middle of the night the convicts, hoping to gain points with the guards, begin some childish anti-German antics. Even though they are really nothing more than fellow-sufferers, their Polish hatred demands expression even in this situation. And so they form a little chorus and bawl their taunting songs:

"The Germans wandered through the woods,
met a bitch and took her for sausage!
Oh, the damned Germans..."

A soloist pipes up:

"The Germans so much water drink
that their asses start to stink!"

The choir:

"A German died, he died
in the street and rotted.
No one wanted to mourn him,
so pigs came and grunted over him...
A Pole died, he died
in the meadow and did not rot.
Three virgins came in the end,
took his body on their hands..."

"Quiet now!" one of the prisoners calls. "Time to sleep..."

At that they jump up angrily, and the choir leader yells: "Quiet? You'll get enough quiet soon, you rotten dog corpse, just wait a bit... And anyone that doesn't croak during the march will be beaten to death at the end!" Then he and his fellow convicts begin to shout in unison, bawling a number of well-known sayings, including this one: "What a Pole can drink in one day is a German's lifetime fortune!"

And then: "Where a frog croaks, you'll find a German..."

And finally: "The Germans buy land with their butter, build houses with their cheese, trade clothing for their buttermilk, and live on their whey!"

Then they switch to regaling each other loudly with the latest news from the front. One of them bellows into the hall: "Have you heard the latest? Our ulans are already at the gates of Berlin, the Polish fleet crushed the German one at Gdyngen, and the French have already marched into Frankfurt! That's the end of you Germans for all time, you're going to become Polish all the way to the Elbe River..." But even this unbearable night comes to an end, and in the early morning light they are already being prodded to their feet again.

Once again the first test for them is another running-the-gauntlet, and in the light of day it seems even worse. When they are finally walking across the open countryside again, with the dust enveloping them once more in gritty clouds, a young girl walking beside a women holding a four-month-old infant realizes that the baby must have died a short time ago. The fluff-haired little head hangs limply, and the little arms dangle loosely with the mother's every step. For a while the girl hesitates if she should tell the mother, but when she sees how exhausted the woman already is, she begins cautiously, carefully: "Wouldn't you like to lay the little tyke down under a bush somewhere, in the beautiful green grass?"

"Whatever for?" the mother asks.

"But it's... it's already..." the girl says timidly.

"It's what?" the woman flares up. "It's sleeping... don't you see... it's sleeping..." And she presses the drooping little head against her chest, sees very well that it falls back again right away, but presses it tenderly to herself again, over and over.

Only now does the girl realize that the woman has already lost her mind. "Do lay it in the grass," she says again, "else you're going to collapse soon! Look over there, that's a nice willow bush, the angels will come for it there..."

But the woman shakes her ravaged head and carries her child on and on. Her eyes are wide as on the threshold of death. "I can't leave my child... my first little child... here underneath a bush, just like that..." she whispers, presses the little head to herself, lets it fall back again, presses it to her chest again...

The road they have been traveling since the morning is the road to Chiechozinek, the well-known Polish salt-water spa. Not far from Chiechozinek is the town of Slonsk; as yet this peasant town of Lower Saxons has been left in peace. It is yet to become the Town Without Men. The marching column's Commandant, who accompanies his prisoners on a bicycle, has ordered the guard troops to question all passing soldiers to make sure that they are not deserters. And so this death march is accompanied now by a secondary manhunt, as runaways from the demolished Polish army are already everywhere. The Germans take a small measure of comfort from these many arrests and think, with an inner smile: they're not going to capture Berlin with an army like this!

Steps drag, the dust clouds rise, thirst turns to agony. Two old men collapse almost at the same time. The policemen stab at them with their bayonets for a while to force them back on their feet, but when even that does not prod them, they shrug and leave the two where they have fallen. The entire column passes by them, takes one last look at their faces, which are almost not human any more - so badly has thirst split their lips, so viciously has dust inflamed their eyes and hunger emaciated their faces. Hardly has the last of the column passed them before several shots crack through the air... Whoever falls, dies - that's the law - not only here but in all other such death march columns.

Shortly before they reach Chiechozinek, one young man, Schreiber from Bromberg, asks to be excused for a moment. "Excused - what the hell - crap in your pants!" one of the guards yells contemptuously. "The time of playing the gentlemen is over for you Germans, and it's high time you realized it..."

Aren't they all sick up to here of this life - does it really still take much to make them toss it aside on a scornful impulse? Before one of his comrades can jump in, Schreiber takes a razor blade he had kept hidden on his person, and slashes his throat. The blood spouts in a heavy fountain from his carotid artery, and before anyone can catch him he sinks backward into the dust. There is a sudden stop, the Commandant leaps from his bicycle and runs towards him, foaming with rage: "You damned zwab, do you think you're going to die when you want to, or when I order it?" he roars down at him and kicks him in the side so that he shudders and curls up with every kick, and with every shudder the blood spurts farther from his throat. A few women sob, one shrieks and faints.

"Doctor Staemmler!" the cry passes down the column.

In a few moments Dr. Staemmler arrives. With a great deal of effort he has managed to obtain permission to help the weakest of the prisoners a bit with his medications. Though he was forbidden to take any of his instruments along on the march, he carries a few necessities in his pockets, including some tonics against sudden faints. He kneels by the moaning would-be suicide. The cut is not irreversibly fatal, the artery can still be clamped. Gradually even the Commandant calms down again and even gives permission to carry Schreiber to nearby Chiechozinek. And so four fellow-sufferers take a coat, place him carefully on it, and carry him along like that in the column.

On the large square in front of the main hotel, between the hotel and the mighty fountain, the spa's symbol, another mob awaits them yet again. But here it is primarily the soldiers, and again chiefly the ulans, at whose hands the Germans endure their maltreatment. After all, a larger cavalry unit is stationed in Chiechozinek. To prevent the same prisoners from always fielding most of the blows during these marches through the towns, the prisoners have taken to switching places from one day to the next, alternating between the insides and the outsides of the rows. And so the day always begins on an especially gloomy note for half of them, namely for that half walking on the outside...

For a while they march through the town, through the streets lined by gardens, past many a villa, and finally they stop outside a gate behind which stands a long wooden house. It is a former Polish youth hostel. All eight hundred of them are crammed into this house, the women separately into a few rooms and the men into a large hall-like room. Once again they get nothing to eat, but thank God some still have a few small rations left, even if that makes for only a few crumbs for everyone. After much negotiating they receive one pitcher of water - it too makes for only a scant swallow for each. Before they can finally stretch out on the bare floor they must endure a severe body search. All razors must be turned over, and all pocket knives, as well as all other metal objects, just as the members of the other death march had to at the start. "Anyone who holds anything back will be shot at once!" the guards scream over and over.

Gradually, night falls, and the air in the overcrowded room grows thick again. Nobody may leave here either to answer the call of nature - one more torment to add to the thousand others. But fortunately few of them still have any such needs - after all, where should they come from, without anything to eat or drink? The men let the urine run down unnoticeably, and general weakness obviates any other needs anyway. Only some few unfortunates suffering from dysentery have a dreadful time of it.

By midnight the air has grown so stifling that some prisoners begin to lose their self-control. The signs of madness increase. A couple of prisoners keep shrieking senselessly at short intervals. Dr. Kohnert has posted a few sturdy fellows by the door to keep anyone from rushing outside in a frenzy. This measure saves several lives, for time and again one or the other tries to force his way out. "I want out, I'm suffocating..." yells one. "I'm thirsty, I want something to drink..." yells another. "I want to go home, I don't want to go on..." begs a third. To top it all off, the even more dreadful screams of the women can be heard from the adjoining rooms. But there as well, some invincible ones have joined forces and physically hold those who have surrendered to insanity back from the gate, for anyone who sets foot outside is instantly shot. Even during this night the women cannot make the young mother realize that her child is long dead; she still holds it zealously fast. Every now and then she opens her dress, holds the drooping little head against her wasted breast, presses the infant's shriveled mouth firmly against it and says in a singsong voice: "Can't you see how eagerly it's drinking..."

And so this second night passes as well. The march continues in the early morning, but before the march-out the guards remove the prisoners' handcuffs. This is by no means done out of a sudden merciful impulse, but out of the realization that, when handcuffed together, the prisoners cannot take cover quickly enough when enemy planes approach. Often enough someone tried to go one way while the partner to whom he was handcuffed tried to go in the opposite direction, and often one of a pair stumbled and therefore the other could not get off the road either. For the men the removal of their cuffs is blissful relief, and suddenly everything seems much more bearable. It was high time for their hands as well, for everyone's wrists are raw; the sharp meal edges had dug deeply into their flesh due to the never-ending tugging, and in many cases, due to the dust, the sores have even filled with sweaty pus.

They are now marching towards Nieszawa. The day grows unusually hot, and the agony of thirst is not long in coming. Many of the guards have levied bicycles for themselves, and like the Commandant they ride slowly alongside the column, rest in the vanguard in the shadow of a tree until the last row of prisoners has passed them, and then ride ahead again to overtake it suspiciously. Before they reach Nieszawa the deranged young mother is finally delivered from her torments; suddenly she stumbles a little and drops forward onto her face, still clutching her dead infant in her arms. Those who walked beside her can see right away that she is already dead - the rearguard will have no extra work dispatching her. She had kept walking for her baby's sake until even the last ounce of her strength gave out.

Half-way to Nieszawa German planes approach again, and only few moments later everyone has taken cover in the ditches. "Thank God," says young Gersdorff, "finally..."

"It was about time!" brawny Adelt adds.

"Indeed - otherwise one might almost think the Poles had really taken over Berlin!" mocks Dr. Kohnert, unperturbed as always.

"That's nonsense, of course. I mean the rest period," says Adelt. "We should get an air-raid rest every half hour or so. Many would regain their strength as a reault, and a whole lot more of us might survive this march."

"I just keep thinking about the British," says Baron Gersdorff, as though to himself. "All this blood is on their hands, because if it weren't for their Guarantee..."

"Definitely!" Dr. Kohnert agrees. "The Poles would never have taken the chance of this war if they hadn't been backed by the British Guarantee. An intelligent Polish officer once told me, 'Despite all our megalomania we're not a nation of suicides!' There can be no doubt that if it weren't for England we would have reached a sensible agreement that really addressed Polish and German needs. But now the Poles will lose everything they had - was that really a service of friendship on England's part?"

"That's exactly how it is," somebody lying nearby says quietly. "It was England that killed my sons, it's England that herds us through the dust here, England that forces us to go without water until we lose our minds, it's England that lets us starve here until we collapse, and it will be England that smashes our heads with rifle butts in the end..."

At that very moment the planes scream right over them, and a light bomb explodes nearby. Something whizzes over their heads, and someone tries to suppress a scream - it's the gray-haired man who was just talking about England. A jagged metal fragment protrudes from his shoulder, but it only went in a little way and can easily be pulled out. A comrade does him the favor. The old man doesn't make a sound at the painful wrench and only says hastily: "Give it to me, it's mine..." And he holds it in his hands and says in a tone of tenderness that somehow also moves the others: "A German fragment... from a German bomb..." And finally he hides it under his shirt, against his chest, like something rare and precious...

An hour later, already near noon, the towers of Nieszawa appear. Apparently the plan is to wait for something here, but the only place that can be found for the column to stay is a huge garbage dump on the outskirts of the city. Here the eight hundred are finally permitted to rest, and so they drop with relief onto the ground between the mountains of garbage that fill the entire surroundings with their stench.

12

The Death March of Thorn, Part 2

Efforts to quarter the prisoners from Thorn on the Jarantonice Estate soon showed that the barns that had looked so promising from afar were already occupied by soldiers. All that was left for the prisoners were the horse stables, which were not only covered in meters of horse manure but also mostly still half filled with horses. Only the women were assigned to an empty garage, and they also received enough fresh straw to lie on, but the men were crammed so tightly into the stables that even here not all of them could lie down.

Nonetheless everyone drops where he stands and is soon fast asleep. But this sleep doesn't last long - hunger awakens them again all too soon. Of the *junaki* prowling the surrounding villages and levying food for themselves, not a one thinks of the prisoners - are they to go without even a morsel for this second day as well? Not until noon do some Germans manage to call a few curious spectators, Polish peasant farmers, over to them. "Sell us a bit of bread!" they plead, and offer them their last few zloty.

"We're not allowed to!" the farmers reply.

"A little milk!"

"We don't have any..." say the farmers.

"Some apples?"

"Apples?" They think about it for a long time, then walk away. When they return some time later they are carrying a basket of apples, still completely green, and moreover just windfalls, gathered up under the estate's trees and scornfully rejected by the gentlemen soldiers. "Ten for a zloty!" the farmers say. "Oh, such pious Christians, such believers in brotherly love..." Dr. Raapke thinks.

They buy a few baskets and distribute them exactly. The apples vanish in just a few moments - what a relief they bring to the starving, and they quench the raging thirst a little too. An old coachman watching this meal suddenly shakes his head and walks away, and eventually returns with a loaf of bread. "Give me twenty zloty..." he says compassionately. "Oh, what a good soul!" Dr. Raapke thinks again. "He truly feels sorry for us, but business is still more important, nothing can make him forget that..." The bread is so fresh that it is still hot - poison to their empty stomachs.

Hardly has a policeman observed the deal before he too comes closer, all smiles. "Give me eighty zloty and I'll get you four!" he says amiably. Some of the prisoners advise against this; haven't they already had bad experiences with such helpful volunteers? But the others insist, and once more a collection scrapes together eighty zloty. But the promised four loaves of bread never arrive...

In the forenoon the Commandant calls Reverend Dietrich and studies him with narrowed eyes from top to bottom. "I need an intermediary," he finally says, "with whom I can discuss certain requirements. You will assume this role, but first you will give me your word of honor that you will not try to escape!"

"I give it!" says Reverend Dietrich. "Do I take it that this means that I am now allowed to talk to all the people in my column?"

"But only in Polish!" the Commandant warns.

"Can I also walk between the ranks during the march?" Reverend Dietrich continues, eager to get the greatest possible gain out of the Commandant's oddly magnanimous mood.

The Commandant nods, then adds: "But if you speak even one superfluous word, you'll be the first to hang from the nearest tree!"

"Then I'd like to make a suggestion right away," Dietrich continues, unmoved. "Our women could cook for the guards in the estate kitchen. And if they got some remnants of the dinner, both sides would benefit from the arrangement."

"A good suggestion," says the Commandant. "So be it!"

And that's already a significant gain. Now at least the women will get something to eat, and no doubt they will be able to divert a little of it to the men. But this hope is in vain; while the women do each get a scoopful when the soup is finally finished, it is entirely impossible to smuggle a pot to the men. But even if the women don't get to eat enough, they can at least drink their fill of the water that was used to wash the potatoes...

Already around noon it becomes unbearably hot in the stables, and besides, the old horse manure underneath the prisoners is so hot that they feel as though they are lying on red-hot rocks. The ammonia vapors rise acidly to their faces, and their eyes, inflamed as they are anyhow from the dust, begin to tear severely. Sweat sheets their bodies yet again and mixes with the dust covering them like fine sand, stinging them all over as with needles. After the soldiers feed the horses, they also water them copiously - how all the prisoners' eyes, wide with longing, follow the course of the full buckets! And how the sound of the water pierces their ears when the horses play in it with their lips! "Do give us a bucketful!" cries an old man in despair.

"Polish water, for you?" the soldier jeers. "If the Polish state wasn't good enough for you, you don't need Polish water either!"

When the horses have been watered, he sets the empty buckets carelessly aside. Almost before he has left the stable, some of the prisoners lunge at these buckets. In some of them there are a few leftover dribbles, mixed with soggy chaff, but the stale remains are distributed so that everyone can at least wet his swollen lips. "In the evening the horses must be watered again," says a farmboy who knows about horses, "maybe we'll get another sip then..."

When evening falls the soldiers return and pour oats into the horses' feedboxes. Many of the Germans sneak up unseen and take out a handful and laboriously chew it to paste - but they can hardly salivate any more and it takes almost a quarter of an hour before they can finally swallow.

During their chores in the stable the soldiers cannot resist mocking the prisoners with the latest news. "Have you heard?" says one of them, "there's nothing left of Berlin but a big pile of rubble!"

"Mussolini has killed himself!" a second adds.

"Your Hitler has resigned!" a third continues.

"He's fled to Doorn, to the Kaiser!" a fourth concludes triumphantly.

The Germans have to remain serious in the face of this nonsense - a smile would already suffice to enrage the soldiers and would no doubt cost a few prisoners their lives. As though to disprove the childish lies, the soldiers' last words are drowned out as an entire squadron of German fighter planes roars in from the west and actually drops a few bombs onto troop units marching nearby. The prisoners have this air raid to thank for a second night spent in Jarantonice. Are the *junaki* not yet able to march on, or are they afraid that the raid would be repeated while they are on the road? In any case there is no march-out that night, and they spend that night still in the stables. Just as Reverend Dietrich brings this news to Dr. Raapke, who shares one of the stables with eighty of his comrades, a soldier suddenly steps out from behind the horses and stands in front of the minister, legs apart. "Let me see your Bible!" he says calculatingly.

Reverend Dietrich takes out his Testament and calmly shows the soldier the slim volume.

"That's not the right one!" the soldier insists.

"I don't know any other!" says Reverend Dietrich.

"You don't know - oh - you liar! 'Mein Kampf' is your Bible - not the New Testament!" laughs the soldier.

At last they water the horses again, and again there is a sip of water for everyone. They are lucky this time; one of the horses did not finish, and a bucket is left almost full. The night gradually falls - but the night is worse than day. Is it just the darkness, or is it because they no longer have any measure of time? Isn't any one of these seven hours longer than an entire night normally is - due to the thirst, the hunger, the heat, that turn each hour into a virtual eternity? To make matters worse, the flies have come indoors now, out of the cool night into the warmth, and like a torture dreamed up by the Poles they sit on the prisoners seemingly by the millions, let nobody close his eyes, crawl like fat tired worms into their noses, into their mouths open with thirst...

The least weary among them whisper quietly to each other and seek to pass the time a little faster in conversation. "Here we sit now," says old man Rausch, the owner of a large engraving establishment, whose son was one of the first to be put into Raapke's cell but whom he has not seen again since the night-time march, "here we sit, the factory owner beside the apprentice, the laborer beside the bank director. Here's the real national community which we've always heard about from the Reich - we already have it, we won't need to learn it after we're liberated."

DEATH IN POLAND

"And what brought it about here?" says Dr. Raapke softly. "The fact that they're not persecuting us individually or as a class, but seek to exterminate us as an entire people. Seen in that light, they couldn't have picked a better way to weld us together irrevocably for all time!"

"Hopefully we'll never forget it again!" old Rausch says thoughtfully.

"Tell me," Raapke resumes, "I remember certain stories we recounted during our alehouse-evening get-togethers, in the good old days. You were once right in the midst of the Russian civil war: did the Russians treat the Whites the way the Poles treat us here?"

Old man Rausch ponders a while, then says decisively: "First of all, there was a civil war going on in those days, in other words, the kind of war that's always the most terrible. And the warring sides shot thousands, and let tens of thousands die. But the emphasis is on 'let', because epidemics contributed the most, and not to forget the general starvation. And those people that were shot, were shot, but the kind of tortures that are a matter of course here were exceptions to the rule there, and occurred only in cases where they had caught someone who had maltreated others before the revolution. Whom did **we** maltreat, and whom did **we** deprive of what's rightfully theirs? That's the big difference, and it makes for an entirely different prerequisite... I saw many a column of deportees in those days as well, but by God, I never saw that they weren't even remotely taken care of, and by God, I never saw that they were prevented from taking a drink of water when they marched past wells in the heat of the day! And I never saw women being so inhumanly tormented, and I never saw even the dead being desecrated by the thousands - those Russians were far too good for that, their souls were pure! And when horrible things did take place there, the perpetrators were usually liberated convicts, or in many cases Latvians, and often Chinese - but here it is the people *per se*, the people as an entire nation, the educated elite, almost every soldier, and also many peasants! And the most important difference: here all these things are done to unarmed people, whereas there it was mostly officers who had been caught with weapons in hand..." He has grown noticeably agitated, has old Rausch, and pauses now to catch his breath.

"That's good, my dear fellow!" says Dr. Raapke loudly. "We shall remember that, for the comparison says more about it than a long account of the events themselves! And at the same time it's as unassailable a verdict as any can be, and it brands the Poles as the lowest people on earth this century!"

"I often heard a soldier say," old Rausch resumes, "when a badly injured White fell into their hands and the Red Jewish Commissar wanted to let him die without even a bandage: 'Wrap him up a bit anyway, for God's reward - even this man had a mother who labored to give birth to him!' Have you ever, even once, heard a Pole say something like that?"

"And that is perhaps the greatest disgrace staining the Polish Church," Raapke throws in, "namely, that it did not intervene in even a single case. When a Catholic priest was dragged from his seminary because he was a German, his Superior did not put in a single word on his behalf. When the Cardinal of Posen drove past one of these columns of deportees and some Catholic Germans hung on to his car and begged him for help for the children among their number, he turned his saintly head away without a word. And in one village, when the women fled to their priest for protection from the soldiers, he told them, right in front of those soldiers and with the crudest curses: 'Turn to your Hitler for help, what are you coming to me for...'"

The acid vapors rise, the heat consumes, the flies torment. Every few moments someone moans, and a few cry audibly. Mouths are painfully dry, eyes burn from the vapors from the manure, stomachs cramp in short intervals as if a cruel fist squeezed them.

"And the teachers!" a man who has many children suddenly chimes in. "My children often told me what went on in the Polish schools. Three times a week, for example, there was a so-called instruction hour, which the teacher opened by showing a large picture of the Führer. 'Who is that?' he would ask. 'It's Hitler!' the children cried, 'the destroyer of Poland!' 'What will happen to him if he falls into our hands?' the teacher continued. 'We'll roast him!' some of the children would yell. 'Cut him in pieces!' shrieked some others. 'Grind him through a mill!' still others yelled. And for the entire hour they did nothing but dream up tortures for him - so why are we surprised at the tortures they now visit upon us Germans?"

"And in comparison, which of us couldn't swear to it," Dr. Raapke thinks, "that in the Reich the state truly wanted to come to an honest understanding with Poland? Didn't they, for example, ban all books that had anything negative to say about Poland?"

"Another question they liked to ask the children in the schools," the man continued, "was, why all the Germans wore boots? So they'd have better posture, for without their tall boots they're all weak! the children would answer. And another: What will we do with them after the war? We'll burn them all at the stake! And a third: How many of them can be permitted to survive? As many as will fit under a pear tree!"

Their conversation is interrupted as everyone is startled to attention. Shrill screams are heard from the women's garage - is someone being raped over there, or is it another touch of insanity? Oh, it's just some who have lost their minds, it's just two women who want out at any cost. "I have to go to my children, they're starving by now without me!" one of them shrieks over and over, while the other one suddenly believes that a bomb will strike the garage any second now.

But there as well, a few dauntless ones stand guard at the door and manage to hold the women back, though just barely. Again, brave Fräulein Buller is one of them.

But the shrieks and screams are the straw that breaks the camel's back for the men as well. A number of the psychologically weakest among them suddenly jump up and also rush the door here. "I'm burning up in here!" one of them cries. "My skin is already covered in blisters, I want into the water, I want to cool my burns..." A desperate struggle begins at the door. If these men succeed in breaking out, there is no doubt that the soldiers will fire wildly into the stable at all of them. In the end the last stalwart few have no choice but to beat them back with hard blows. And so they finally collapse, exhausted, back onto the manure. One of them keeps repeating dully, at least thirty times: "Let me at least make a phone call, let me tell my folks at home..."

Finally the first light of dawn glimmers through the windows, and the insanity of the night falls away from them one more time like a spook. Even the most out-of-control are suddenly sensible again and listlessly obey their leaders' instructions. Only one of them suffers a relapse even in the brightness of the morning. When Reverend Dietrich comes to the door to discuss some matter of business, he calls out to him: "There is no God any more, I know it now for certain! Let's pray to the devil instead, my fellow Christians, he alone can help us here!" And he continues in a sermonizing tone of voice, "This world belongs to him alone, all people serve him alone..."

For a second, Reverend Dietrich stares at him helplessly, then walks over to him decisively, takes a big swing and slaps him resoundingly in the face. "Shame on you," he cries, "you call yourself a man, and talk such nonsense? Pull yourself together, like those weaker than you manage to do..."

This sharp blow, these sharp words, they act like a cold bath. The madman stumbles back, rubs his hand over his forehead as though waking up, then drops weakly onto the manure and breaks down into desperate sobs.

And again the sun rises, again the hunger begins, again thirst torments them all. Again they purchase some apples and drain the dregs from the horses' water buckets. Reverend Dietrich has won the concession that now the prisoners may be led out to answer the call of nature, but hardly anyone still needs to. On the few occasions when the gate is opened for such a reason, the prisoners see the *junaki* sitting outside, stuffing their faces and feeding the dogs with their surplus. Oh, if only they had these leftovers, how happy they would be... But nobody begs, not even now - as yet their pride has not deserted them, and their souls are still stronger than all the tortures their physical bodies can suffer...

As dawn breaks, the order comes to march on to Wloclawek.

13

The Death March of Bromberg Joins With One from Pommerellen

Hardly have the deportees from Bromberg settled down on the garbage dump of Nieszawa before an even larger column of deportees enters the street leading to this dump from the west. It numbers well over a thousand people and also includes many women; apparently it is coming from Pommerellen.

For the first time the Brombergers see a sort of mirror image of themselves as they observe a death march column like their own. Certainly they have encountered many others by now, but only ever in a hurried march-past while they themselves were also being herded along. Here they now lie resting on the heaps of garbage and for the first time they really have the time to absorb this devastating sight, never to be forgotten: The first sign of it is a slowly advancing cloud of dust, next they begin to hear the constant yelling of the guards, and only then do the first rows of deportees appear. The first rows are usually made up of those prisoners who are still in the best shape, but the longer the column marches past, the more bent are the backs of its members. One old man hangs with his arms draped across the shoulders of two others, reminiscent of an old eagle with dragging wings; his once clear eagle eyes are almost lifeless and only his bent hook nose gives an indication of what his face may have looked like before all this. Many other men virtually hang in the elbows of their comrades, their legs dragging on the ground rather than taking steps. Many of those who are carried on in this manner by the sacrifice of their fellow marchers move their legs more like puppets, in the air, only skimming the ground with dangling toes. But as long as one even just goes through the motions of walking, his ethnic brothers do not desert him...

When the Brombergers finally also look at the passing faces, there are few among them that do not wonder: do I look like that too? These deportees as well have not washed for eight days, and so the layer of street dirt, grown loamy with the sweat of marching, has formed a finger-thick crust over their features, giving the faces a rigid look, like mummies. Since many also have bleeding wounds from the many blows, this loam is often marbled with blood, and looking out of these rigid masks are eyes which are frequently also suffused with blood, and always badly inflamed for days already. But the gaze from these sick eyes is something the watchers will least forget: In most of them the gaze is already almost dead, vacant as the eyes of the dying, but many still have the expression of hunted game; after all, isn't all this just one huge hunt? Their clothes are also unspeakably ragged; the men's suits are uniformly gray with dust, but out of a poignant sense of decency some still wear their collars, even if for a long time already they have just been wrapped around their necks like gray rags. In a few cases they are even still held together with neckties, like they used to be in better days. As for the women's clothes, except for those traditional peasant dresses of tough linsey-woolsey they are the most tattered of all. The light summer fabrics have been reduced to rags, the older women's hems have been uniformly trodden down, the thin silk of the young girls' blouses is riddled with holes, and bright blood runs down many of the women's bare legs. But the saddest aspect of all are their feet, for most of the prisoners no longer have shoes. And so they have wrapped their feet with handkerchiefs instead, or in many cases only with scraps of coarse sackcloth which they were fortunate enough to find somewhere. All these unshod feet are bleeding from the march and often have been covered in pus-filled sores for days already - no matter how many thousands of steps they must take each day, they still flinch painfully with every footfall...

"So that's what we look like!" Baron Gersdorff suddenly says. He and the column's leaders sit at the foot of a great heap of ashes, reclining against their bulk. Even Dr. Kohnert's lean face that almost always wears an expression of cheerful self-assurance is as though shadowed from within at this sight.

"So that's what we look like!" Adelt repeats quietly. "But unfortunately nobody else sees it, and nobody else ever will see us like this. The English politicians should sit here in our stead and miss one of their Sunday visits to church - maybe just once their unctuous words would stick in their craw and they would realize, even if just for a moment, their own culpability!"

"Or some of those pious Misses who love to go work in the missions to help poor Negroes to the blessings of Christianity!" Dr. Kohnert says sarcastically. "Here they would have a grand scope indeed for their Christian compassion and could earn themselves a choice seat in Heaven..."

"What keeps going through my mind these days," Adelt suddenly bursts out passionately, "is this, first and foremost: Whatever may happen to Poland during this war - whether all her cities are destroyed by it, whether her entire intellectual elite is wiped out in the various battles, whether a third of her people die in the iron hail - I cannot imagine any consequence of war that would strike me as somehow unjust: If a people can deal in such a way with unarmed fellow citizens, none of what it may receive in return can be undeserved, and any and all it does receive is only just! And when the great humanitarians from abroad come along and throw up their hands in horror and cry: poor Poland, look at what all was done to her - it is up to us to point out calmly as often as it takes: it was all fair and just - whatever was done to her! For what Poland herself did here, what she has done to countless civilized human beings which she herded through the country like so many heads of cattle, how she drives us here and others there, that is such an incredible crime against civilization that there can be nothing, nothing at all which this nation may ever have the right to complain about in the future, for her own actions have disqualified her from the elite of civilized nations! And after all, when the time comes that she pays the penance for her actions, she will not pay it for the acts of individuals, since the entire people, the entire nation was to blame for this gruesome mass murder and participated in these inhuman tortures of innocent people, beginning with the Marshal of this State, to the vaivoda and professors, to the teachers and down to the most uneducated peasants, from the officers down to the last soldier! Neither the women nor even the children of this 'chivalrous' people have remained free of blame for this mass murder - all of them have soiled their hands with this blood and reveled in the torments of the defenseless! Neither the world nor this nation herself had better complain about the penance it will one day have to pay for its sin against humanity - God himself will not hear it then, for these deeds have also defiled God! And if philanthropists of all colors should one day turn to bestow their care on this nation, then speak to them of nothing but these deportation columns - if you tell it right, and tell nothing but the truth, then no doubt they will soon see for themselves that this people, this nation is no longer deserving of love and that their good deeds are better served on anyone else than on Poland!"

They are all somewhat surprised by their comrade - it is generally not his way to come out of his shell with such passion. And then they turn their gaze back onto the new arrivals. Their column is slowly nearing its end - it has been led onto the same dump site, by the way; perhaps they will even continue their march together?

"All of this is true," Dr. Kohnert finally says. "But I already know today exactly what the other nations will say to all of this: Hardly had the war broken out before the Germans staged a huge ethnic uprising, for they had been well armed by the Reich! What else could the poor Poles do but get rid of them as quickly as possible - seeing as now they were being attacked not only from the front, but also from within! The fact that their anger at this treacherous attack led to some excesses, well, who could possibly blame them for that? A small nation fighting for its survival in the same situation will always act like this!"

"My God in Heaven!" Adelt cries out in shock. "Now it's suddenly become clear to me why the arrests were always accompanied by searches for weapons, why they claim the Germans shot at them from every house, and why they planted rifle cartridges wherever they could! Your explanation shows the overall plan, prepared in advance from higher up, and with every means at their disposal... That's the story that was put about amongst the entire population, and most of them probably honestly believe it..." He stops, devastated, and puts his head in his hands. "Isn't that horrible?" he asks softly. "Have there ever been statesmen before who did something like this, so lightly? We are not the only ones who have to suffer so terribly under its consequences - the Polish people will also have to face dreadful repercussions. And all of it is lies, just a satanic deception...?"

"But nobody will believe us, and that's the bitterest part of all!" Dr. Kohnert speaks up again. He has discovered a broken spoon among the rubbish and pockets it as a valuable discovery.

"But that's impossible!" Adelt objects, agitated. "After all, everybody knows what oppression we endured, that it was impossible for us to have weapons, that almost daily house searches had not left us in peace for half a year already, and that the discovery of even a makeshift weapon meant months in prison! And also that the borders had been hermetically sealed for months already and so even smuggling something in would no longer have been possible! How should we have managed to arm ourselves, when all old weapons had long been confiscated and new ones were not to be had? It's simple fact that not one of us could have shot at the Poles because none of us Germans had a single weapon left - it's a perfectly clear-cut case - the truth *has* to win out..."

"Well, I still doubt it," says Dr. Kohnert, unimpressed. "In our century the truth is no longer absolute, but rather a function of who has the greater propaganda apparatus."

At that moment, a prisoner arrives whom one can just barely recognize as a clergyman. Two surly Poles accompany him. He is the Reverend Krusche, the leader of the newly arrived deportees. They hurriedly discuss the most important things, but are forbidden to speak further; nonetheless they have guessed it anyway: both columns are to continue their march jointly from here on. Meanwhile the leaders of the Bromberg deportees have recovered enough that they can tackle the most pressing matters their role as leaders entails. Dr. Kohnert has a guard lead him to the Commandant, whom he asks for permission for some of the prisoners to buy some bread, with their own money. Strangely enough, the Commandant permits it this time. Zloty are hurriedly collected again, and the hope travels like wildfire: "There's going to be bread, we're going to get some bread..."

By now the newly arrived deportees have settled in, and now there are almost two thousand people lying among the trash. Even though most of them lie still, a cloud of ash constantly surrounds them, since even the slightest movement stirs up the dust. Many of them kneel among the garbage, poke through it searchingly - maybe there's an old crust of bread to be found, or even a head of cabbage someone has thrown away? These wretched figures grubbing through the filth are the most devastating sight of all; over here, one gnaws greedily on a moldy crust, over there another one has found an old tin can, which he happily attaches to his jacket with a piece of wire. Now he finally has a drinking cup - all that's missing is the water! But most of them lie among the piles of garbage as though struck down, only moving their pus-encrusted eyes when someone else drags himself past, and moaning with parched, split lips for a drop to drink.

The dump lines the street along its entire length and is separated from it only by a guardrail surrounding it on all sides on three-feet-high posts. To the right of the street is a tall board fence which evidently encloses a sawmilling square; to its right are a few sandy hills, with some wretched peasant shacks standing on it. Not far from this little ridge of hills, on the other side, stands a Protestant church, and not far from that stands a small house, just across the street from the dump. Here, it seems, lives an ethnic German family that has not yet been expelled.

And from this house they receive the most marvelous gift they could imagine under the burning midday sun: Suddenly a petite woman steps out of the doorway, her straight black hair falls in pageboy style to her shoulders, and at her side there walks a brightly chattering little girl - in either hand, however, the bashfully smiling woman carries a bucket of water! There is almost a stampede among the prisoners, and it takes the leaders' combined energy to prevent them from simply running the little woman down...

And so they drink, almost all of them, and even though each only gets a mouthful, that mere sip goes far towards reviving their spirits. For three hours this diminutive woman - she is the wife of the sexton Wiese, who has fled - carries her heavy buckets from her house and across the street, and when the prisoners' purchase of bread also arrives from the city, the general happiness almost knows no bounds.

At four o'clock in the afternoon, far too early for everyone's liking, the order is given to march on. Once again the deportees organize themselves into columns and rows. The group from Bromberg is the first to leave the dump site, after which the group from Pommerellen heaves itself out of the garbage as well. A cloud of stench follows them for a long time yet - a reminder of the time they spent lying among the trash. They march along close to the banks of the Vistula river, towards Wloclawek, which they just manage to reach by nightfall. Eyes wide with surprise, they see that many houses here have already been shelled, and again they nurse some hope of being liberated soon after all. All of them are crowded into a gymnastics hall, but no matter how large the room is, once again there is not nearly enough space for all of them to stretch out on the floor. But here at least there is no garbage mixed with human excrement on which they must huddle, and there is no stinking street dirt mixed with sharp glass shards on which they must stand barefoot.

Very early the next morning the march goes on, but no longer eastward - suddenly they are directed to move south. Could it be that the Germans are to the east, that they have already blocked off the roads? Dr. Kohnert manages to obtain one more concession, namely that some ill men may also ride on the carts along with the sick women. But when seventy-year-old Superintendent Aßmann, a dignified minister with the best of reputations, asks for the same privilege, it is difficult to preserve him from bodily harm. "Look at this gangster," the Commandant yells, "how harmless he acts, and yet he's the most dangerous of all!" And so two young men take him on their arms again and all but carry the exhausted old man this entire day as well. Finally the entire column is moving again as before, with dragging feet, enveloped by dust clouds, beaten in every village they pass through, spat at - or more - by everyone they pass...

This day as well soon grows hot, almost like a summer's day, and the sun beats down mercilessly on the traveling prisoners. As they have had nothing to drink since leaving Nieszawa, by noon their thirst approaches lethal degrees. Often there are large water tubs standing by the roadside; these have been thoughtfully placed there by farmers for the passing soldiers - but the prisoners are forbidden on pain of death to drink from them. This midday the death threat no longer has its intended effect; an old man is the first to suddenly throw himself over such a water tub and, forgetting everything around him, he drinks insatiably. But even while he is still drinking, and others are about to follow his example, the nearest guard leaps towards him with his gun barrel in hand, takes a huge swing, and already the rifle butt crashes into the back of the old man's head. The man does not make a sound; his head, half-crushed, sinks into the water, and his upper body slowly follows while the clear water turns red with his blood. "Have you got enough now, you damned water guzzler!" the policeman screams at him. He does not even permit the lifeless corpse to be pulled out - no, it is to remain in the tub, as a warning to others...

Towards evening the first cases of delirium occur; some of the prisoners begin to hallucinate. "Over there, that's my estate, and at the gate, my Elisabeth, she wants to give me a pitcher of water, just let me go to her for a moment!" a young farmer keeps crying out. If one of these unfortunates does not happen to have someone walking in his row who still has the strength to hold him back, his remaining lifespan is measured in seconds. For anyone who takes even one step out of line is immediately beaten to death by the guards.

More and ever more of them begin to see hallucinations - marvelous rivers with waterfalls, surrounded invitingly by shady stands of trees: "Just a few more kilometers! You can already see it clearly, just up ahead," they say to their comrades, in all seriousness. "Muster up just one more time, we'll be there in half an hour!" Around five o'clock these delusions become so strong for some of them that they suddenly break ranks and run with long strides towards a nearby hill. Immediately, wild shooting begins, and none of them make it farther than ten meters. After they fall, every one of them is stabbed to death with the guards' bayonets; in his rage one of the guards even jumps on top of one of the prisoners, stands on him with one foot on his throat and one on his private parts, holds his carbine reversed and aims one stab after another into the writhing body. Three *strelzi* wearing their heavy nailed boots jump the prisoner who made it the farthest towards his hallucination, and viciously trample his face until there is nothing left of it but a bloody pulp...

One after the other drops back from the foremost ranks, falls back row after row until finally he has arrived at the back of the column. There, the nearest guard seizes the opportunity to kick him in the back - if he holds up under this he may live a little longer - usually he collapses under the third kick, which tends to follow the first very soon. That, however, is the signal for his liquidation, and thus he ends the same way as all the others before him, under a rifle butt. Forty-four of the prisoners already half dead from thirst die in this manner this day...

But things are still progressing too slowly for the Poles. Which of them would ever have thought that these Germans would be so tough? Just outside Chodez the Commandant runs into an officer, a well-dressed, well-manicured first lieutenant from a Warsaw regiment. He dismounts his horse for a moment, exchanges cigarettes with the Commandant, and finally the stranger says, with a tilt of his head: "Why are there still so many of them? On the entire march here, haven't you even had the time to clean up a bit among these pigs?"

The Commandant just laughs and squints his eyes. "That's all still to come, don't worry. I prefer doing it slowly!"

At that, the other laughs as well, and presses his horse on: "That's right, that way they'll get more out of it too, those damned Hitlerowzi..."

At long last the sun sets, dusk falls. "Just a bit more patience," a young farmboy among them keeps repeating to himself, "soon the first dew will fall..."

But even before the dew falls and they can lick it up, they arrive at their day's destination, the large sugar refinery in Chodez.

14

Towards Warsaw: The Death March of Thorn

In Wloclawek the deportees from Thorn are herded into the same gymnastics hall where the Brombergers had also been quartered, except that the group from Thorn spends the day there instead of the night. The *junaki* still continue the practice of marching at night, whereas the *strelzi* have already given up on that. Once again they do not get so much as a bite to eat this day, and not a drop to drink. And so, despite their exhaustion, the prisoners long for the time when they are to march on again; perhaps there will be an opportunity outside to take a sip of water from a puddle somewhere. Maybe it would even rain - how wonderful that would be! One could simply march along with one's tongue stuck out, head thrown far back, one could let the rain run into one's mouth for hours like that...

But when they are let out again, they see to their disappointment that the stars shine brightly in the sky above. Certainly, at least there is some dew, but they are not allowed to step out of line and not even to bend down. Well, perhaps there will be an air raid soon, then they will have to take cover in the ditches where they could stick the damp grass into their mouths and cool their mucous membranes a bit, swollen as these are from the dryness. But even though the moon is bright there is no sign of any planes, and so hallucinations soon begin among this group as well. One prisoner thinks he sees lush melon vines growing in the ditch - isn't there one of the juicy fruits hanging from every bush? "If only I could get over there, if only I could bend down even once," he says to his neighbor. "I'd have one with a single grasp. The vines are full of them..." He glances cautiously around, but one of the guards is walking right behind him and so he staggers on for a while, keeping his head always turned towards the ditch. Finally he can't bear it any longer and leaps in... The guard fires the same instant. A few times the prisoner's hands still grope through the tall grass, searching for the illusory melons... "Trying to escape, are you?" the guard yells and repeats his rifle. "I've been watching you the entire time, you damned dog corpse, but you won't get away from me..."

Finally, in the third morning hour, a few planes approach, and immediately everyone flings themselves into the ditches without even awaiting the order to do so. How cool the grass is, and how wet it is! Some of them bury their faces in it, others stuff great handfuls of it into their mouth. And - what bliss - the ditch adjoins a turnip field! As unnoticeably as possible they all pull one out, and an arm full of leaves as well, those are so heavenly to chew and the pulp is like balm to their inflamed mouths! And so they are saved for another few hours, saved by the German fliers - gratefully they gaze up at the grey eagles thundering eastward above them in the pale moonlight.

For a few hours they all enjoy some relief, but then the same old torment begins anew. Almost everyone now walks with arms interlinked. That way the ones in the middle can almost sleep while they walk, for their legs move all but automatically by now. And everyone also sleeps during even the briefest of stops, some of them falling so soundly asleep that they do not hear the bellowed orders to resume.

If ever they are ordered to sit down, they all drop instantly wherever they happen to stand, whether it be in ankle-deep dust, in the manure of livestock that was herded past, or in the blood of someone who had been shot. None of it matters, just lie down, right away, immediately, don't lose even a second...

Reverend Dietrich patrols the entire marching column several times each night, led by a sullen guard. He is like a loyal shepherd solicitously circling his herd. Whenever he sees someone in one of the rows who totters all too noticeable and has nobody left to either side of him strong enough to support him, he leads him to the end of the column himself and helps him onto one of the sick-carts. Often he notices, the very next time he approaches the cart, that the one he had helped onto it last time is no longer to be seen, but he is not permitted to ask what happened to him. Does he really need to ask anyway, don't the shots that one hears so frequently at the end of the column say it all?

But only few of them still die by a bullet; most die by the bayonet. If a *junak* happens to feel tired, he simply goes to one of these carts. If there's room for him there, good - if not, he just pulls the nearest prisoner off and sits down squarely on the cart instead of him, while his cronies "liquidate" the sick prisoner, stab him a few times and then simply roll him into the ditch. In this way there is always enough room on the carts for the sick, and despite the constant influx there is only ever the same number of them...

Even at night the roads are now buzzing with peculiar activity. Thousands of peasant carts head eastward along with their column, and in between, entire livestock herds travel along, bawling hungrily. Frequently the prisoners recognize vehicles from Thorn which the refugees have simply commandeered; trucks from the municipal waterworks alternate with street sweeping vehicles, milk trucks from the German dairies follow delivery vans from companies whose owners are staggering along themselves among the ranks of the deportees, and once they are even passed by a factory owner's splendid car in which a whole number of them had enjoyed countless holiday excursions. It seems that all of western Poland is heading east and hardly a Pole has remained in the old German provinces.

"That's their bad conscience!" says old Rausch with a certain measure of satisfaction. It seems this old Siberian's strength is endless, even though one thing torments him constantly: He has not seen his son for days. Perhaps he managed to flee, but perhaps not...

At the next stop he espies an auxiliary policeman who had used to work in his factory for years. He calls him by name, and the guard comes distrustfully closer. "You know me, I used to be your boss - tell me, was I ever not good to you? Didn't I help you often?"

"You did!" says the auxiliary policeman, looking cautiously about.

"Now listen... Here you have my gold watch, and I only want one thing from you in return: Tell me what happened to my son! You know him, you used to work with him..."

The Pole squirms, sneaks a covetous glance at the watch, and finally says softly: "He's dead..."

Old man Rausch flinches a little, is silent for a while, then hands the Pole his gold watch and says: "Now you must do one more thing for me, you must shoot me dead as well. No, I don't want to live among you pigs any longer, now that you've even shot my son... Come, take it, don't be shy - but take me as well, right over there is a nice tree..." And the Pole takes the watch. But he does not let old Rausch leave the column, says instead in a hushed voice: "I'll try to find out where your son was left..." and steps aside, walks back along the road...

As the column finally approaches Kutno, they run across countless troop units marching in as reinforcements. But even these fresh units are not troops any more in the German sense of the word;

something has already shaken their inner sense of confidence and they no longer have their entire strength and resolve. Maybe they won't be able to push us through after all, the abductees think with renewed hope; maybe we'll end up in the midst of battle? One air raid after another is being flown on the Kutno train station, but even though they march through the city not far from this station they never once feel real fear: It's not aimed at us, they think, almost child-like, they won't hit us, not our German brothers... In many places the houses are already on fire and line both sides of their nocturnal way like gruesome torches. The crashing thunder sounds to them like the drumroll of the Last Judgement.

Near Kutno they are once again herded onto an estate. This time an old cow shed is their lodging for the day. Again there is nothing to drink, except the contents of an old concrete basin that has filled with drip water from somewhere. The bottom of this basin is lined with old manure which has colored the water yellow, like tea, and besides, there is not even enough for a sip for half of them - but how the others envy those that get such a sip! Around noon Dr. Raapke manages to persuade a farmer to sell the group a large pitcher of milk. When he finally brings the container, bought at dear cost for many zlotys, the milk consists of two-thirds water, but at least now those who did not get a sip of the manure tea can have a bit to drink as well. An hour later, Reverend Dietrich manages a great coup: he buys a pig from the estate owner himself, for an outrageous price. In great haste the women go to work, the pig is butchered, scalded, and already it is cut into small pieces and cooks in a large vat. During the cooking time the prisoners are virtually seized by a fever of anxious anticipation; will the soup be done in time, or will the guards order them to march on just before?

They are not driven on just before, as they had rightly feared; on the contrary, the guards even wait accommodatingly until the meat is well done - but hardly is this meal, the first soup since eight days, ready, when the *junaki* boldly move in. "You've cooked a good soup for us!" they taunt, pull out their dishes and sit down around the stove, grinning broadly. Almost all of them help themselves to seconds, wolf the meal down with lots of lip-smacking - and then they throw the dirty dishes to the women to wash, and bellow the dreaded words: "March out..."

Hurriedly the women at least fill all the containers they happen to have, and even have an opportunity to carry the leftovers to the men in their shed - but it is too late for them, and only few of them can still fill their tin cans. Not one has the time to eat while they are still on the estate. When the huge column, somewhat delayed by all this, does not line up as quickly as usual, a policeman walks up to the vat and kicks it over. "Now you'll move a bit faster, no doubt!" he yells, and chases them out of the shed with his pistol.

That night they march to Dobrzelin where they are housed in a sugar refinery, a huge, state-of-the-art industrial structure. Here they have a lot to suffer at the hands of the laborers, who have clearly been incited to hatred against the Germans and once more supply them with all sorts of "news from the front", of the same tenor as always. What does it matter to these vapid illiterates that a third of Poland is already occupied and that almost all active armies are fleeing as fast as their legs will carry them?

They remain in this sugar refinery for only two hours; already the order is given with great anxiety and excitement to move on. They are to spend this day in a nearby forest, an announcement that fills even the last of the five hundred with profound joy. Finally, to spend some time again in real daylight, not having to lie crowded together like sardines on filthy boards, not being eaten alive by flies. "No doubt the *junaki* fear an air raid," says Dr. Raapke, "otherwise they wouldn't be so agitated!"

But they do not even make it to the forest. Halfway there, a counter-order reaches them: "Fast march to Zychlin station!" they are suddenly told. Fast march, the abductees think - what do they call what we have had to do so far? No, it hadn't been a fast march so far, they realize that the very next moment: from all sides the guards begin to beat them, until the five hundred literally are running. Almost instantly this saps the last strength out of many of them who might yet have endured days of marching the old way - dozens of them drop on the road to Zychlin, and behind the column the rifles do not fall silent for even an instant. The crack of the shots acts on the remaining prisoners like whip lashes, driving them forward time and again despite their weakness; perhaps they finally will be put into cattle cars in Zychlin, perhaps the torture will finally be over there? The vague knowledge that they are heading towards a train station carries many of them through some deciding moments; without it, hundreds would have fallen and died on this stretch of road...

And indeed, in the station of Zychlin there is a freight train, with its steam already up, and even a few passenger cars are coupled to it. The men are crammed into the freight cars, sixty-two per boxcar, but the women are in fact led to the passenger cars, where they can actually sit down for once. From here it is merely a hundred and twenty-five kilometers to Warsaw; they could be there in three hours. Finally the train moves out, but it is delayed for a long time at almost every blockade.

Due to all this standing time in the searing sun, the temperature soon soars to tropical levels, and sixty-two people soon use up the air in their confined space. And once again there is nothing to drink, nothing to eat... During one stop at a track inspection station Dr. Raapke manages to call a boy playing on the embankment over to the train. "Bring me a pitcher of water," he says to him, "I have so many sick people here in the car..." The boy hesitates for a long time, but finally he brings a bottle of water and says shyly: "One liter - one zloty..." Someone has a sort of egg-cup on him, and this is now used to divide the one liter into sixty-two tiny portions which, thank God, means half an egg-cup for everyone! Even if it's not enough to drink, it's at least enough to soothe a little, to soothe the swollen tongues and cracked lips...

But this ride as well ends unexpectedly soon. It is more apparent with each passing hour that the Commandant does not really know what to do any more. Is the train almost encircled already? Is the Commandant trying, by means of this back-and-forth, to break out somehow? After only fifteen kilometers on the train they are chased out again, in the middle of nowhere, and are again fast-marched to Leonzyn. Once again dozens fall by the wayside, but now they are no longer shot, due to the noise; they are now silently beaten to death. In the town of Leonzyn they are quartered, for the first time, not in a stable but in a fire hall, in whose huge outbuilding they discover, with wild amazement, a huge hydrant.

A drinking spree begins such as none of them had ever dared dream of: moans of pleasure fill the entire room, some of them let the water literally run into them, nearly choke on it, almost all of them conclude by taking a final mouthful which they do not swallow for a long time but hold in their mouths to cool the mucous membranes. Drinking is followed by another pleasure, that of washing their swollen feet - in long rows they sit on the stone floor, a bowl or some other sort of vessel full of the cool water beside them. Slowly they peel the rags off their mangled feet, some of which have had the flesh worn off literally down to the bone. Almost everyone's toes are little more than a mass of pus. How good the cool water feels, how unspeakably good it feels... After everyone has cleaned their ulcerated sores as best they can, they tear the last good shreds out of their shirts and carefully bandage up their poor mutilated feet once more... Even if hunger still gnaws at them, at least their thirst has been quenched and the worst of the raging pain in their feet has been soothed - now if only the Reverend could obtain some food from town...

But this time even the Reverend fails, and they must march on that very same night without having had a bite to eat. Not far beyond Leonzyn is the river Bzura; for a while the Commandant searches for a ford, since the large bridges are hopelessly jammed by the troops. After a while he finds one where the water is only just over two feet deep, and the five hundred are fast-marched through. "If we'd had such a crossing a few days ago," many say to their neighbors, "no doubt all of us would have thrown ourselves in for a moment!"

For the first time the deportees see fleets of destroyed vehicles at this ford, a battery and dead horses lies in the Bzura, and peasants' abandoned escape vehicles lie scattered everywhere. Again the night is brightly moonlit, and it is gruesome to gaze at the pale faces of fallen soldiers whom the deportees have seen more and more frequently for the past hour... Were there battles here already? they think with renewed hope. Indeed there were battles here already, but a day earlier, a day too soon for the prisoners; but again they are lucky: just one hour later the ford is already under German artillery fire! Only one hour later the Battle of the Bzura would have crushed all five hundred of them...

But even though they are now close to Warsaw, they are still not safe. (See Appendix, Photo Document 17.) Every few hours they must change their direction. If the Commandant were not such a good field soldier they would no doubt already have become stuck in a dead end somewhere. Fortunately the murderous pace has slowed as well; it was the *junaki* themselves who protested against it because despite being well-fed they could not keep it up. They rest briefly once more on the Lomna Estate, a model estate owned by the brother of President Moscicki, and that night they see flashes from the artillery on the horizon, on either side. Again they march in sharp angles, once to the right, once to the left, and again the Commandant manages to evade the combat area. Gradually the sound of the machine guns fades, the roar of artillery diminishes with every kilometer, and now it can't be much farther to Warsaw. "So it seems he got us through after all!" says old man Rausch, resigned. "He would have done better to show his skills at the front, than here with us poor sots..."

They spend the day in the town of Blonie, and from there they are to march in one shot to Warsaw - aren't those the city towers that they can already see in the hazy distance?

15

The Death March of Bromberg: Finally, Freedom in Lowitsch

Part of the sugar refinery of Chodez, a large industrial complex that has already been in ruins for years, is surrounded by meters-high barbed wire. When the Brombergers are herded into this part, they see with surprise that there are already approximately two thousand deportees there. Evidently the factory is a collection camp, and together with them it now holds some four thousand. But even as they enter they realize that not all of them are ethnic Germans - roughly a thousand are Poles, some of them old Social Democrats, some hopeless Communists, some simply convicts. Nonetheless these give the arriving Germans an undifferentiated welcome: a shower of spit rains down on them from the sides, a filthy flood of curses washes over them. "Why are they still dragging you here anyway?" one of them shrieks in a voice that drowns out everyone else. "They should have butchered you right where you were caught - just like we're going to do to your Hitler in Berlin!"

The prisoners are forced into a narrow space between the walls of two destroyed factory halls whose window panes have all fallen out, whose floor is covered partly with liquid tar, partly with large chunks of sharp-edged coke fuel. Here they are permitted to sit down, shoulder to shoulder, back to back, as they are used to sitting by now.

Civilians wearing armbands stumble around among them and inform them, amid curses, of the rules of this camp: "Anyone who approaches the barbed wire will be shot immediately. Anyone who leaves the spot assigned to him will also be shot!"

"A straight-forward camp order!" says Consul Wenger bitterly. He is a German consul, an old Privy Councillor, and has a diplomat's passport - but what good is international law to this old gentleman here; he is driven across the country like everyone else.

In the evening all the deportees are suddenly sorted according to the color of their arrest tickets. This gives rise to vague concern for some - could it be that the holders of tickets of a certain color are going to be shot here? But after this sorting has gone on for hours, everyone is suddenly chased back to their old places in no particular order at all. Nobody has thought to provide any food for these four thousand human beings, but they are given something to drink once before nightfall.

The night itself passes quickly, even though the prisoners are bitterly cold in just their shirt sleeves, but this time they at least have fresh air to breathe, and only sharp stones underneath them rather than hot manure.

March-out is very early the next morning, and the four thousand are all herded out together. The destination is Chodzen, a small country town full of Jews. These too curse the prisoners to no end, while others offer them goods for sale. For a while they can make some purchases from these, until suddenly the *strelzi* drive all of them away with much yelling - and shortly thereafter they offer the Jews' wares to the prisoners themselves, though now at twice the price. Did they simply take the goods from the Jews, or did they buy them from them in order to profit their own pockets - what do the starving deportees care, at least they can still buy a bite to eat!

After this short stay they march on without stop until just beyond Kutno, the occasional air raid being their only opportunities to catch their breath. During one such raid they happen to lie near a well, and those closest to it can hear its gurgling stream of water. Almost all of them close their eyes so as to hear this wonderful sound even more clearly, all open their parched lips in longing.

"If we could hold on to this, this gratitude for just a sip of water, what more evil could possibly befall us for the rest of our lives?" Adelt suddenly says, in his straightforward manner.

"Don't worry," says Dr. Kohnert skeptically, "it'll all be forgotten again!"

They march on for ten hours, they march on for eighteen hours, they march on for twenty-four hours. Just as for the deportees from Thorn, this is the last great forced march, intended to avoid encirclement at the last instant. One more time the prisoners' torment grows to unspeakable severity, time and again the foremost rows thin as one after the other falls back to the rear. In the fifteenth hour of the march they begin to drop in huge numbers, and even Dr. Staemmler is beginning to lose the last of his strength, though he still patrols the column up and down, rendering assistance wherever he can, while the *strelzi* often beat him severely for it, despite the agreement to the contrary.

"My tongue feels like a piece of wood in my mouth!" even the indomitable Dr. Kohnert finally says. It is the first and only time he says such a thing.

"I'm beginning to see sparks!" admits burly Adelt.

"I'm gagging, as though I had to throw up..." says young Gersdorff softly.

In the twentieth hour of the march an old minister, who so far had miraculously survived everything, also dies. He sinks slowly to his knees, folds his hands and gazes over the wide countryside that is spread out in mournful beauty before him. "I don't want to go on," he whispers with white lips, "please, call me home now!" And he adds, almost bashfully: "Forgive me these words, oh Lord, but Your Earth is not beautiful..." He closes with the words: "For fifty years I have served You... but now I no longer understand You... why did You, in Your goodness, create such people?" And at these words the rifle butt strikes him, his white head of curls turns suddenly red, then two guards grab him by the legs and drag him into the ditch.

The roads are still dominated by troop movements, some coming towards them and some passing them at breakneck speed. Since the roads are hopelessly overcrowded, the prisoners usually have to march beside them on the fields, and the dust clouds from the light soil rise to mountainous proportions. Once they pass very close by some plowing farmers who, strangely, do not curse at them but look them in the eyes with great sadness.

"Those are Germans!" one of the prisoners says incautiously. And already one of the *strelzi* has heard him, whips around, yanks his rifle up, shrieks in a shrill voice: "What's that you say - still more Germans? And not here with you, not prisoners?" Shots ring out. One of the farmers falls across his plow, the panicked horses drag him wildly away across the field. The other farmer falls in the furrow, his legs twitch a few more times before he slowly stretches out on the soil.

Great confusion reigns in Kutno. What a contrast to the slogans that scream boastfully from almost every wall: "Every threshold is a fortress!" "Every house is a Polish stronghold!" "Every Polish child is a hero!" In truth there is little left to be seen of such heroism - it all degenerated into an orgy of Slavic sadism long ago! At the corner of a house decorated in this manner, two prisoners suddenly jump in front of a truck; they too do not want to go on, they too prefer a quick death to an evidently endless martyrdom. The truck rolls over them with a sharp crunching sound and drags both of them along for a short distance, but at least they do not die under the blows of rifle butts.

After twenty-four hours of marching they get their first real rest; on the Starawies estate everyone is permitted to lie down for four hours in a barn. They do not get anything to eat here either, but at least everyone receives enough to drink. They all lie on the ground gasping for breath, many of them are seized with heart spasms - whole rows of them die of exhaustion here, flickering out like tired candle flames. Wasn't this one over here just talking to his neighbor? Now he suddenly stretches out with a sigh while his eyes glaze with a milky veil...

When the march resumes at four o'clock in the afternoon, the entire barn floor is dotted with black lumps, but the *strelzi* first walk up to these lumps, stab their bayonets into each one just to be sure... The estate's farmhands are ordered to bury the dead that very same hour. It seems that they have buried one while he was still alive, since the soil dumped on him still moves for a long time afterwards; another one is dispatched when they slice his belly open as though butchering a pig, tear his intestines out and stuff a dead dog inside him instead.

Once more the abductees must march without rest for eighteen hours, and now their ranks thin even more than before. Time and again they must shuffle to make up their number per row again. "The Pole just collapsed," whispers Dr. Staemmler when he returns to the front of the column. "You remember him, he stood by the side of the street in one of the towns we passed through and was the only one to show disapproval of how the crowd treated us, and so they simply pushed him into our midst. 'But I'm a Pole!' he kept yelling. 'If you stand up for the Germans you're no better than they are!' he was told. All his pleading did him no good, and so he had to march on with us to this day - well, just now he ended under a blow from a rifle butt exactly like so many of us..."

Strangely enough, the column can still cross the Bzura on a bridge - probably because they are crossing this river farther to the south. As the vanguard has reached the middle of the bridge, one of the men walking in the first row suddenly leaps out of line and jumps off the bridge, seven meters down into the water. A whole handful of guards instantly fires at him, but not one manages to hit his target - who wasn't trying to escape anyway, all he wants is a drink. And so this seventy-year-old farmer, Koerber, calmly rejoins the end of the column after he has drunk his fill from his hat.

Are we going to get through? Will the Commandant manage to get us through? is gradually becoming the only thought buzzing through the heads of the three thousand. The Commandant himself shows no signs of concern. He rides alongside the column on his bicycle as always. But as of yesterday he has dreamed up a new form of devilry, whose fiendishness the prisoners do not realize for quite some time. More and more frequently the Commandant rides up to one marching in the column, suddenly puts his arm around his shoulders, very friendly, and strikes up a pleasant conversation with him. "Well, how are you holding out?" he says with a smile.

"Oh, thanks, Commandant, I'm managing all right..." The prisoner freezes inside - could it be that the Germans...?

The Commandant puts his arm ever more tightly around the prisoner's neck while at the same time driving more slowly - so that his victim has no choice but to slow down, to fall back more and more from his row, to let the rest of the column pass him. "And do you have any children?" the Commandant continues.

"Two, Commandant, two boys..."

"No doubt you're looking forward to seeing them again?" he asks, smiling.

"And how!" says the German disingenuously. He feels the Commandant's arm ever more heavily around his neck - what's the meaning of this, he thinks with growing bewilderment.

But already they've arrived at the end of the column, and the Commandant abruptly draws his arm back and with pinched lips he calls out to the rear guard: "Away with him..."

It takes no more than that for the German to understand. "Oh," he has just enough time left to cry, before he falls...

The Commandant, however, quickly cycles back to the front, skims the rows with narrow eagle eyes, chooses another one around whose shoulders to put his arm, and says in a tone of warmth and sincerity: "Well, how are you holding out?"

And begins to drive more slowly...

It takes four hours for the deportees to see through this new method, and from that point on everyone follows the bicycle's progress with staring eyes. "Is he coming for me... for God's sake... is he looking at me?" Many already begin to tremble when they just see him from afar.

"Everyone put their glasses away!" the message passes quietly from row to row. "It seems he's only choosing people who wear glasses, he's probably hoping to wipe out the educated ones among us," whisper the prisoners to each other, "since in Poland wearing glasses is already enough to be considered educated!"

When they already see Lowitsch in the distance, they also hear the first machine gun fire - artillery fire has already thundered around them for hours and they have long grown used to the howling of the shells. The pace they are expected to keep up is growing more and more unbearable; even Dr. Staemmler is beginning to stagger, and gradually even the strongest start to hallucinate. Suddenly, courageous Adelt suddenly cries loudly, *"czolo stac"* - and in the very next moment everyone is flat in the dirt in the field. It is the Polish command for "vanguard stop"; in the general confusion nobody notices that this time the order was given by a German. By the time the counter-order comes, they have all spent a few minutes lying down, and even these minutes were enough to preserve some of them from imminent collapse.

An hour later they reach the city of Lowitsch and stop near the barracks, while grenades crash explosively into the houses all around. The Commandant leaves to make inquiries, and most of the guards follow him. They remain at this rest stop amid the artillery fire for half an hour until suddenly some policemen chase them on.

"The Commandant isn't with them any more!" the whispered news travels through their rows. "Maybe we've been encircled after all, maybe he's taken to his heels...?"

The policemen lead them out to a little forest, but there all their hopes collapse again: whole hordes of *strelzi* stand in front of the grove, all of them have their rifles in hand - are they waiting for them for the final massacre? "Up that hill!" the policemen scream. The order fills the prisoners with insane dread as they suddenly feel that even while they are running up the hill the *strelzi* will mow them all down! The hillside is exactly in their field of fire, that's why they're standing at the ready here...

"We're not going on!" a thousand voices abruptly cry as one.

"We have to try to negotiate..." Dr. Staemmler exclaims.

"That's exactly what I will do," says Dr. Kohnert calmly. "Just come with me," he adds, and approaches a nearby policeman. But when the Pole sees the two coming towards him, he begins to wave his gun in the air.

"For God's sake," cries Dr. Staemmler, "he's going to shoot us..." And with these words he leaps the last few steps towards him - all he wants to do is to knock the rifle barrel aside, but already the Pole pulls the trigger - shot through and through at close range, Dr.

DEATH IN POLAND

Staemmler falls onto his back, and is dead before he draws his next breath. The policeman glances only briefly down at him before he flees as fast as he can to the *strelzi*.

At that instant a tank appears at the edge of the forest and rumbles directly towards them. Dr. Kohnert turns to the Reverend Krusche, the leader of the second column, and says with a strained smile in his voice: "Well, come along, Reverend, this is our last march! At times like this it's always good to have a minister along!"

Deep inside he still does not give up hope; no doubt this tank is going to crush them now, but maybe, if he can only negotiate quickly enough... And so he pulls out his last handkerchief, waves it over his head for all to see, and walks with calm, firm steps towards the tank, while the entire column crowds along at his heels.

But hardly has he taken a dozen steps when he suddenly feels as though his heart would burst - this tank bears a white cross, this tank is a German tank! No, he is not mistaken - written on the tank's front, in German, is the proud name "Ziethen" - and already it stops, the turret opens, a young officer leaps out...

In the next moment the prisoners also recognize him, and hundreds suddenly fall into each other's arms, sobbing and kissing each other's bloody faces...

* * *

One hour later they are all quartered in now-occupied Lowitsch, showered with all sorts of blessings by a hundred caring field soldiers. The eighty-year-olds are cushioned on clean straw; one among them is well-known Dr. Busse, one of the most famous livestock breeders in Europe. His white-haired, wrinkled head is covered with blood-suffused black blotches, and bright blood trickles from his split lips. Lying beside him is an eighty-two-year-old plant nursery owner from

Schönsee, but both will survive despite all they went through, and both will be back home in just a few days.

Only one of them will not see his home again; he lies in a small room, silenced forever. And this one man is the devoted doctor who, in his constant patrolling of the column, walked the entire distance of this death march probably three times over and who saved hundreds of lives with his medications and ministrations - Dr. Staemmler - who, after miraculously surviving a thousand deaths, died at the very last instant, in the face of the first German tank.

16

The Death March of Thorn: Through the Hell of Warsaw - to Freedom

That same morning the deportees from Thorn set out from Blonie to reach Warsaw in one final march. Their original destination had been the fortress of Modlin, but here they already got caught between two fronts and therefore diverted northward in great haste while the grenades shrieked across the sky over them. At two o'clock the towers of Warsaw rose before them in the early afternoon haze, and at four o'clock they arrived in the park of the Ojzow Marianny Cloister.

Under the trees they are granted a brief rest, then they enter the first suburban street and march towards the northernmost bridge in Praga. But as they approach the suburb of Praga the Commandant realizes, just in time, that its streets are already a battleground; the barking of the tank guns is clearly to be heard. They are rushed back through already-destroyed streets and finally reach Warsaw proper in the Jewish Quarter of Nalewki. Here the streets are black with caftaned Jews, who soon realize that the new arrivals are a column of deported Germans. Promptly they beat at them furiously with their umbrellas, spit at them in loathing as if in a ritual prayer - and yet their antics strike these seasoned sufferers as almost comic. "We've survived worse!" old man Rausch comments.

He is doing this day's march beside a man who cannot be much younger than himself but who, like Rausch, is still continuing on his way with surprising vigor. "I was friends with a man in Thorn," he says, "who had already gone through the same thing once before in Siberia. I heard he's among our number too. I wonder if he made it."

"Who is he?" Rausch asks him.

"Old man Rausch", says the stranger.

"But that's me!" the old Siberian cries, and adds, "and who are you?"

"I'm Bruck!" says the old man. "You're Rausch?" he then repeats in amazement. "And we're walking side by side here - and don't even recognize each other - though we're really the best of friends?"

"You're Bruck?" Rausch shakes his head, he too can hardly believe it. "That's a good example," he says after a while, "so that's what we poor sots look like, so bad that even our best friends no longer recognize us!" He clears his throat, then continues: "But that we found each other just at the very end, that's nice despite everything, isn't it - because I can't shake the damned feeling that there's something special in store for us yet! But together we can get through that too, don't you think..."

His premonition was correct. For a while they still need to make their way through the Jews; they hardly pay any attention to their shrieks of abuse, some even have to repress chuckles at their behavior. More than anything else, the barefoot prisoners enjoy the asphalt they feel under their tired feet for the first time in what seems like ages. God in Heaven, what a relief it is for their injuries - no more grinding dust, just a wonderfully smooth surface that feels like a cool compress against the soles of their feet. Despite their utter exhaustion they suddenly walk along with new energy; after this strange relief they will no doubt survive the last assault as well.

The Jewish Quarter is behind them, the first barricades appear, and thus begins the final chapter...

* * *

The barricades consist of all sorts of vehicles, sometimes of overturned streetcars, often only of stacks of huge crates, and on top of them stand not only Polish soldiers but also crowds of civilians. Already as the deportees move through the first of the narrow passageways that were left open in the center of the barricades, an ear-splitting yelling and screaming begins among those on top.

The same instant projectiles begin to crash down on the prisoners from all sides - a dense hail of rocks, a thousand sharp-edged pieces of wood. The people have lined up with incredible speed at the passageways to make the prisoners run the gauntlet, and strike at them with slats and boards quickly pulled from the roadblocks themselves. The most dangerous blows are those aimed down at the prisoners' heads by the people on top of the barricades.

"Give me your arm, Bruck!" Rausch cries hastily. "If we link arms it's easier, we can each support the other! Wrap your jacket around your other arm and hold it over your head..." The two old men just barely have the time to get ready somewhat before the crowd pulls them through the narrow passage as well. A younger man right in front of them suffers a blow from a soldier, who smashes him in the face with a frying pan so that the blood gushes in a wide stream over his chest, but his comrade helps keep him on his feet at the crucial moment of collapse. The two old men make it past this roadblock without major difficulty; it is not until the third barricade, already deep inside the city, when they can already see the open prison gates, that old Bruck is hit severely over the head.

"Up, man, up!" cries the Siberian. "We're almost there, just stay with me a bit longer, just another twenty steps..." Old Bruck's knees are about to give way when he hears his friend's shout and feels his comrade drag him on with the last of his strength...

"Run!" someone yells. And they do, they actually begin to run one more time - the last surviving five hundred run gasping towards the gate, pump their tired legs once more across the asphalt, whipped along by fear - but a whole number of them are no longer capable of this final exertion and they collapse despite their comrades' help, they collapse under the blows still being rained on them from all sides, their last spark of life goes out in the very face of the beckoning prison gate that would have meant their safety.

In the prison yard of the Dzielna they all drop to the ground, wipe the blood from their battered faces and try to catch their breath. "Well, in any case, we have arrived at the end of our march!" says old Rausch, gasping for air. "There's no way they're going to get us out of here again, since evidently Warsaw is already completely surrounded..."

Most of the others have the same impression, and so their spirits lift surprisingly quickly. If only they're not forced to march any more, everything else will be a hundred times easier to bear! Even if their captors should give them nothing to eat, even if they put them all in dark-cell arrest, as long as they don't have to run any more on their ulcerated feet... After a while they are divided into groups of ten, and all groups are taken to the Women's Prison. The cells there are intended for only three inmates, but nonetheless they are no more crowded there than they were so far. And when there is a real meal in the evening - a liter of soup for each, soup in which it seems some meat had been cooked! - this night strikes them as the best one since their arrest.

The next morning they are taken from their cells again and actually led to a shower. For the first time in weeks they can peel the clothes off their bodies, a bliss that only someone who has ever been in their situation can possibly comprehend! Many of them also take off their shoes here for the first time, for due to the sudden march-outs nobody dared take them off during rest breaks after many had lost theirs in the beginning, during the hasty departures in the dark. And so they return to their cells clean for the first time. The prison staff even took their laundry away, to be washed, and it is to everyone's amazement when they actually receive it back, clean, two days later.

The old marching buddies have managed to get themselves assigned to the same group, and so they are together again in the same cell. Dr. Raapke even has a few cigarettes left, but unfortunately only a tiny number of matches. But when someone finds a pin, one old prisoner immediately knows what to do: He divides each match into four parts with the pin, and so they now also have enough of these for many a day. It is also this same old ethnic German pioneer who helps to while away the endless days by telling his cellmates about other prisons in which he spent long times, with interruptions.

"We can consider ourselves lucky that we were brought here," he says one time. "If we had ended up in Bereza-Kartuska, that infamous Polish concentration camp, they still have methods of punishment there such as we Germans haven't had since the Middle Ages... For example, when someone is sentenced to dark-cell arrest, his underground cell is also filled with a foot of water so that he can't even lie down for days.... If someone commits an offense against a superior, he's tied together with arms and legs at right angles so that a broomstick can be inserted under his elbows and the backs of his knees, and the broomstick is then hung on a tall rack so that the prisoner hangs from it head-down. Then they tie his mouth shut and force water into his nose through a hose until he passes out from the pain, and then they beat him on the raised soles of his feet until he comes to again from the pain, and then the procedure begins all over again... At the interrogations they use an electrification device, they hold one of its contacts to the prisoner's nose and the other to his chin and then they send heavy charges through the device so that it slams the prisoner's jaw shut each time with downright primordial force. Many of them have bitten their tongues off that way..."

The prisoners shudder; some of them get goosebumps. "Truly a nation of culture!" Dr. Raapke finally says. "And I know for a fact that many of us were there, and no doubt there are hundreds there right now who share that same fate..."

Old man Rausch jumps up in agitation and cries, in his impetuous manner: "After all that's happened, who could expect the Germans in the border provinces ever again to live on a close neighborly basis with the Poles? Isn't every Pole in those border regions at the very least a relative of one of those murderers to whom each of us has lost members of our families? And didn't each and every one of them participate in it all, at least mentally and emotionally even if not with their own two hands?"

"You're absolutely right!" Dr. Raapke says decisively. "Nobody can ever again expect that of us. Not only our own people, but the other nations as well, have to acknowledge that! The Bloody Sunday of Bromberg, the starvation death marches, Bereza-Kartuska - with these three monstrosities Poland has cut itself off and made all neighborly coexistence impossible..."

"Do you believe we'll win?" an old man asks timidly.

But Dr. Raapke only smiles, and says with calm certainty: "Who do you think will win? The Poles, perhaps? But a nation that was able to do what was done to all of us can never win honestly, you can take my word for that... And besides, we're going to win for entirely different reasons too, for reasons that are beyond all matters of military potential, beyond all strategies and beyond all blockade theories: There is only one law that applies without exception and always comes into force, and that's the biological one! England is old, France is old, Russia is young, Germany is young - but in the long run it is always the young nations, the revolutionary peoples, that emerge victorious! We are the revolutionary part of the world, and that part will win in any case because in doing so it only complies with natural law - Poland has foolishly thrown its lot in with the old part of the world, and for that reason it will be destroyed, because feudal states must perforce always give way to socialist ones! And after all, this war is not a struggle for power in the traditional sense, it's rather a struggle of the poor nations against the rich, and as an uprising of peoples it's the same thing for the world that the social revolutions of various classes were for individual peoples; just like their struggle for the more just distribution of goods within their national borders, this is the struggle for reorganization among the haves and have-nots on a global scale! In 1918 the reactionary forces, the haves, won one more time but in the long run it is always the revolutionary forces that win, whether they be revolutionary in an intellectual or in a material sense - and in that respect this second world war is not even, in essence, a war, but in a much more decisive respect it is a great revolution!"

They all remained silent for a long time, until at last someone says softly: "Your theory is absolutely correct, and if it were not to come true, history would no longer make sense!"

After the first few days passed quickly, the next begin to drag on and on. At times an odd-job man manages to pass them news from the front, but these are usually so contradictory that it takes a lot of skillful reading between the lines to get at the core of truth in them. Fortunately for the prisoners, they continue to hear the distinct sound of artillery fire; this way at least they know that the German troops are still holding their old positions. Very nearby the prison is a heavy Polish anti-aircraft battery, and from the fact that it is put into action almost hourly they happily deduce constant German air raids. At the same time, however, the presence of this battery is an disadvantage for them in that the German artillery persistently aims for the flashes from its muzzle, which means that heavy 15-grenades detonate regularly in their vicinity.

Initially, the women in the Dzielna have a harder time of it than the men, but they too can finally get themselves cleaned up right after their arrival. A compassionate woman whose clothing barely still reveals that she is a deaconess immediately resumes the chore she has performed so many times before: bandaging the many sore feet. The daughter of a master locksmith is in especially bad shape, and the entire soles of her feet are one seething mass of watery blisters. The deaconess washes them carefully, and gradually the girl's toes reappear from under the filth.

"Oh, what is this," the deaconess suddenly says in surprised alarm and stares at the girl's toe nails, which are a bright, garish red, "could it be blood-poisoning?"

But the girl blushes deeply and says with suspicious haste: "Oh, no, it's nothing..."

At that moment another young woman walks past; her name is Trudy, but everyone calls her "Little Sunshine". She is a "painted woman" well known throughout her home town and was also one of the deportees, but everyone soon honestly came to like her because she did not lose her courage for even a moment. "Would you like a bit more polish to re-paint them?" she laughs. "Despite all that's happened I still have the bottle with me..." And not a few of the other women smile and think, this girl will probably never in her life paint her toenails again!

Already the next day, however, all of them are ordered to report to the laundry room, to launder incredible masses of convict clothing. And there they must stand now in the heat and the steam for twelve hours a day. Some of the laundry is already crawling with worms, while other clothing comes from the field hospitals and is often stiff as a board with dried blood. But even this work has its little joys, such as when they occasionally discover a shirt belonging to a prisoner, labeled neatly inside: Private Meier... After a week even this work must cease, since the water supply is cut off. That same night they hear wild yelling outside in the streets, and despite some pistol fire things do not calm down again. The following day an odd-job man tells them that there have already been hunger revolts in the city, since there is no more bread to be had in all of Warsaw.

During these days the quality of their rations quickly deteriorates. The first thing to be lost is the soup, then there are no more potatoes either, and finally all they still get is a kind of bean tea, a pale liquid with a few lone beans floating in it. These are also the days that claim the lives of a few more elderly people; the worsening rations virtually knocked them down, and one prisoner dies of dysentery which also suddenly breaks out. By now it has been some fourteen days that they have spent here; in the beginning it was bearable, but nobody will last much longer under these conditions. Again the gnawing hunger makes its appearance, as does the everlasting thirst - no food is supplied to the prison, and the water mains are still broken...

Just as they are about to lose the last of their hope, an incredible bombardment begins. "That's the final phase!" cries Rausch enthusiastically. "Now we just have to get through this, and then Warsaw will be in German hands!"

The old Siberian prisoner was quite correct. For two days thunder crashes all around them, as though the earth were bursting and being reborn. Almost all the window panes explode, and the thick walls vibrate more and more severely. Occasionally one of the grenades also hits the prison, but once again the cellblock in which all the ethnic Germans are imprisoned is spared - not one of the thousands of detonations does any serious damage here. Eventually everyone's eardrums ring to the point that they can no longer hear a word anyone says; some show signs of losing their minds again, and one of them begins to preach: "I am the Lord thy God, I shall deliver thee, so it is written..."

All of a sudden the awesome bombardment ceases, and after one final infernal crescendo dead silence falls. "Now they're overcome, now they're showing the white flag!" the prisoners think. An agony of tension grips them all - what will the next hour bring? But for several hours more, nothing at all happens; then, late in the evening, their cell door is suddenly flung open, and a Colonel stands at the threshold, white-faced. "You are free," he says simply, "you can go..."

Who could possibly describe the reaction to these words? But Dr. Raapke soon calls for common sense and urges the over-eager ones to reconsider and stay until morning. So they spend one more night in their cells and are properly discharged in the morning. Meanwhile, Reverend Dietrich reports to the army headquarters and returns around noon with a Major who is to guide the deportees through the Polish front line. And so they finally march out through the devastated city of Warsaw. All the streets are full of piles of rubble, and some houses look as though they had been blasted from the inside, with only the outside walls left standing. Occasionally they see half-eaten horse cadavers, torn-down streetcar cables above them, and in the old battery positions lie heaps of corpses. Around four o'clock in the afternoon they near the front line at Mokotow; dozens of burned-out tanks lie scattered throughout the surrounding area, and between them, entire rows of battery teams. In the middle of the battlefield they are instructed to wait, while Reverend Dietrich and the Major go on ahead to the German front line.

An hour passes - three hours pass - darkness falls. The deportees crowd together like a herd of sheep, the women in the center. The night grows freezing cold for them in their thin shirtsleeves. The moon rises in silent brightness, and in its light they can see hundreds of returning Polish refugees who were evidently turned back at the front. Since they are huddled on top of a hill, they can see far across the Polish countryside: its sad beauty extends sweepingly to the horizon, broken only occasionally by a pale white birch. In the distance, fog descends quietly over a village, its wretched wooden huts sit on the ground as though cowering timidly in the lap of Mother Earth - but one and the same night sky arches over the watchers as over this village, home to the same yellow moon on its silent passage, and the same stars twinkle on its blackness like silver tears.

Finally, around midnight, the minister returns, everything has been arranged, and now they can start on their final journey. With every hundred meters they put behind them, the battlefield becomes more gruesome. Dozens of white horse cadavers lie everywhere, toppled cannons with gaping muzzles between them, and on top of some of these, overturned gun carriers whose loads of grenades are spilled all around. Stubby chimney remnants are all that remains of the houses that once stood here. Countless burned trucks fill their yards, and the entire area is permeated by such a ghastly smell of decomposition that many women moan softly at the sight of this dreadful scene of destruction.

"Woina na woina!" says the Major who guides the deportees' passage, and shrugs tiredly. *"C'est la guerre!"* the French would say - "That's war!" Yes, it was - this was war, exactly as they saw it here,

to their horror, on their last night-time march to freedom... But this sight not only fills them with dismay, it also announces to them the overwhelming victory, the devastating German victory over Poland to an extent which they had not dared hope for in their wildest dreams.

Finally, as they approach a village, the vanguard sees a troop of soldiers - aren't those German soldiers? And suddenly all sense of marching order is forgotten, the rows spontaneously disband, the entire column breaks into a run...

And then the first of them stand before the soldiers, look at them with staring eyes: the gray uniforms, the brown leathers, the old steel helmets! And a few young girls throw themselves into the soldiers' arms and break into such unrestrained sobbing... as though they could never stop again.

* * *

When Reverend Dietrich took the first head count, he found that one out of every five prisoners in his column had lost their lives on these Polish roads. In and of itself that was not a huge number, but hadn't there been countless other such deportation columns, being similarly herded through the country? And didn't each and every one of them lose hundreds of members, after thousands had already been killed in the cities before? Hadn't the Poles even shot thousands of German soldiers in their own army, even though they had always loyally done their duty? Weren't farmers killed behind their plows, mothers while nursing their infants, even children at play?

The fate of a few was discovered. The fate of tens of thousands will never be known. In countless places the vast expanses of this country had become a German graveyard, and Poland's roads are lined for all time by its invisible crosses.

17

Postscript: 65 Years Later

"But I already know today exactly what the other nations will say to all of this:... *What else could the poor Poles do* but get rid of [the German minority] as quickly as possible - seeing as now they were being attacked not only from the front, but also from within! *The fact that their anger at this treacherous attack led to some excesses, well, who could possibly blame them for that...*"

That was what Dr. Kohnert predicted in September 1939 (Chapter 13). And how did reality turn out? The following article from February 3, 2003, published in a prestigious mainstream German news periodical, gives a glimpse:

> "Poland
>
> ***Compensation for Death Sentences?***
>
> The Federal Republic of Germany is facing a new wave of ***demands for compensation for Nazi crimes - this time from Poland.*** Before the Wehrmacht marched in to the city of Bydgoszcz (Bromberg) in September 1939, the city had been the scene of attacks by Poles on members of the German minority (in Nazi-speak: "Bloody Sunday of Bromberg"). After the occupation, Nazi judges quickly passed several hundred death sentences, which were usually carried out immediately. ***Surviving family members now hope to***

achieve the legal vindication of those who were executed. "The sentences were passed in a perversion of justice and must be rescinded," says Cologne attorney Andrzej Remin. German authorities had paid up to 10,000 Marks compensation in a similar case two years ago. The money went to the surviving family members of the defenders of the Polish Mail of Danzig who had been sentenced to death by National Socialist courts and for whom Günter Grass created a literary monument in his book *The Tin Drum."*

(Translated from: *Der Spiegel,* February 3, 2003. Original at https://www.spiegel.de/spiegel/print/d-26270950.html)

Any further comments would be superfluous here.

Scriptorium, September 2004.

18

Appendix: Photo Documents

The photographs as well as their caption texts are taken from the book *The Polish Atrocities Against the German Minority in Poland. Edited and published by order of the Foreign Office and based upon documentary evidence,* published in 1940 by Volk und Reich Verlag, Berlin. In the caption texts, "RKPA." indicates findings resulting from the investigation of the Special Police Commission of the Criminal Police Office of the Reich, while "OKW. HS. In." indicates autopsy and post mortem findings.

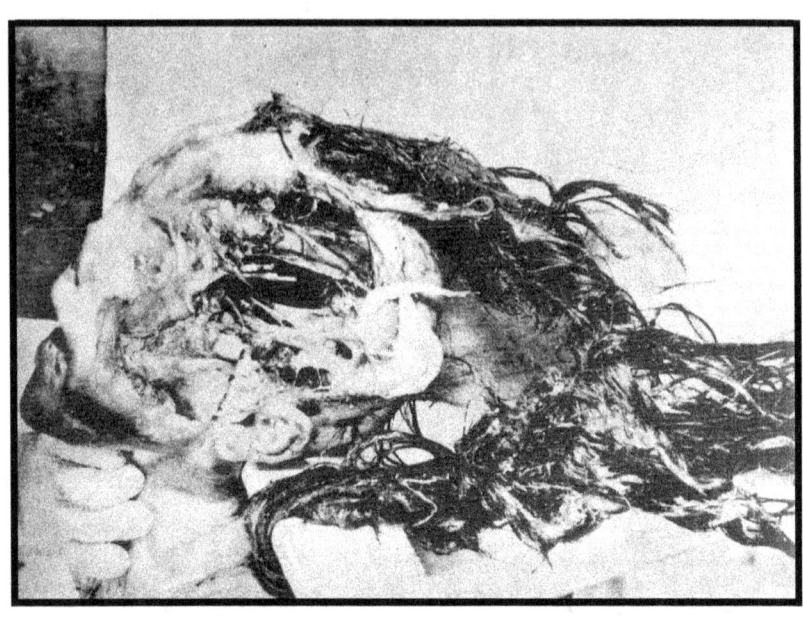

Mrs. Frieda Ristau, 31 years old, one of the group murdered in Eichdorf-Netzheim; mother of 3 children who were fortunate enough to escape being murdered. Skull blasted by gunshot fired at the back of her head.
Sekt.-Nr. - Br. 88 (OKW./H.S.In.)

Photo Document 1

Ground floor and exposed basement rooms in the Schmiede house, totally gutted by deliberately set fire. Sixteen people had to endure the heat for eight hours in the basement because the windows were being shot at. Not until later could the ethnic Germans crawl into a different basement room, whose ceiling was of concrete. Schmiede himself and two other persons who came out of the cellars were shot dead on leaving the burning building.
Tgb. V (RKPA) - 1486/19. 39

Photo Document 2

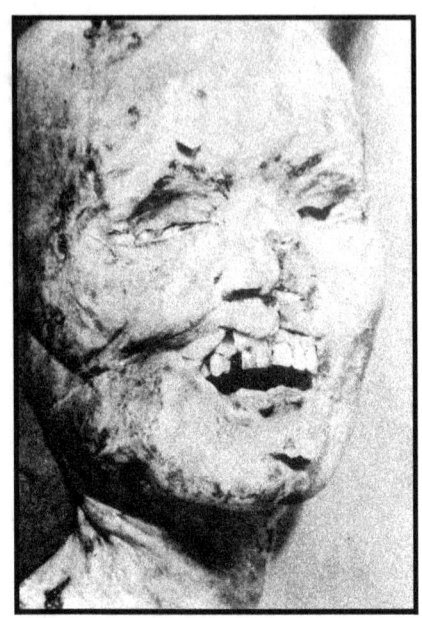

Fritz Radler, 19 years old, member of the murdered Radler family. Blow from bayonet or sword to chin and near right eyebrow. Fritz Radler was killed by a shot to his chest with a Nagan revolver; the bullet remained lodged in his chest.
Sekt.-Nr. - Br. 48 (OKW./H.S.In.)

Photo Document 3

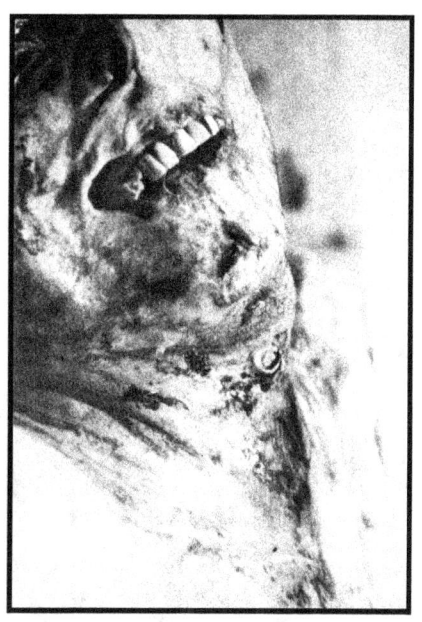

Arthur Radler, 42 years old, member of the murdered Radler family. Bullet entry hole in throat at the left. The corresponding exit wound is at the back of the neck, at left. The injury was not immediately fatal and Mr. Radler suffered for more than 7 hours. His wife and 14-year-old daughter were prevented from helping the badly wounded man. He was eventually killed by a shot to the head.
Sekt.-Nr. - Br. 46 (OKW./H.S.In.)

Photo Document 4

Foreign doctors listen to the eyewitness report of 14-year-old Dora Radler from Kl. Bartelsee near Bromberg about the murder of her father and both her brothers. Left to right: Dr. Espionsa (Chile), Dr. Karellas (Greece), Dipl. Ing. Santoro (Italy), Dr. Faroqhi (India), Dr. Ohanian (Persia).

Photo Document 5

Heinz Beyer, 11 years old, and assistant gardener Thiede.

Photo Documents 6 & 7

Gardener Friedrich Beyer.

Kurt Beyer

Photo Documents 8 & 9

Kurt Beyer's shattered forearm - detail from above.
Sekt.-Nr. - Br. 100 (OKW./H.S.In.)

In Thorn Street in Bromberg the bodies of 10 ethnic Germans were discovered, beaten to death and mutilated.

Photo Documents 10a & b

German farmer's wife from Langenau, near Bromberg. Her right foot was cut off and then her leg was separated, butcher-fashion, from the thigh.

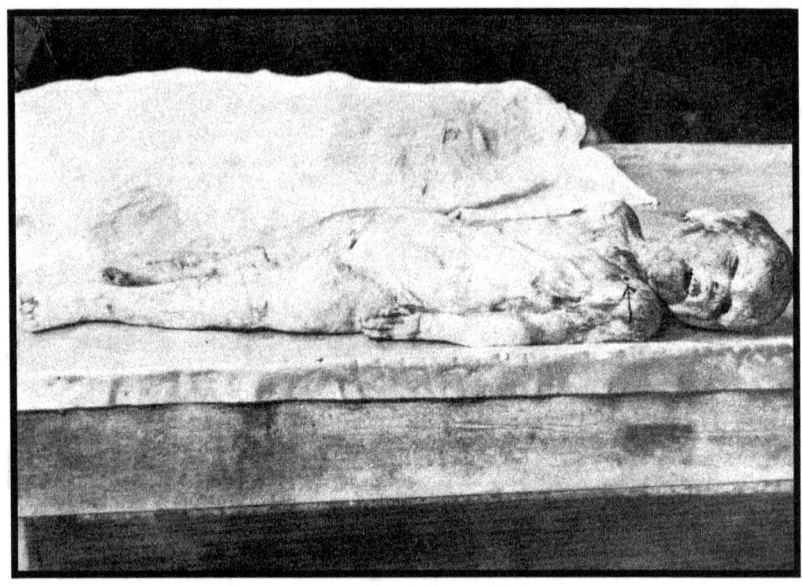

Erhard Prochnau, 3 years old. One of the group murdered in Eichdorf-Netzheim. The nanny, Johanna Schwarz, 45 years old, was murdered along with the child. Bullet exit wound in the lower left clavicle. The corresponding entry wound is in the upper right shoulder blade area at the same height of 71 cm. The horizontal course of the bullet at such a low height indicates that the child was shot in the arms of his nanny.
Sekt.-Nr. - Br. 76 (OKW./H.S.In.)

Photo Document 11

Livestock watering hole in the forest of Targowisko, into which the bodies of 15 murdered ethnic German children, women and men were thrown - together with an animal cadaver.
Tgb. V (RKPA) 1486/3 39

Photo Document 12

Unknown man, approx. 40 years old, one of the group murdered on Jesuit Lake. Explosive nature of bullet exit wound in face proves the weapon used was a rifle. The murdered man was one of a sub-group of Jesuit Lake victims, 12 men who were tied together with livestock ropes.
Sekt.-Nr. - Br. 21 (OKW./H.S.In.)

Photo Document 13

Willi Heller, 19 years old, one of the group murdered on Jesuit Lake. 33 stab wounds from daggers or bayonets; the arrow indicates the fatal blow which damaged the spinal cord in the neck.
Sekt.-Nr. - Br. 23 (OKW./H.S.In.)

Photo Document 14

Example: after a house search. The home of Raiffeisen Bank manager Symosek in Gnesen after 20 Polish soldiers ransacked and looted it. Symosek was carried off together with his two daughters, Eva aged 19, and Dora aged 16. The soldiers stole a large sum of money from the desk and all of Symosek's suits, including clothes laid away for the winter. The Iron Crosses (1st and 2nd class) and other of Symosek's war decorations were thrown into large washbasins, the latter then being used by the soldiers for relieving themselves.

Photo Document 15

Murdered ethnic German farmer from the town of Langenau near Bromberg.

Photo Document 16

Ethnic Germans outside Warsaw, shot and beaten to death en masse. Bodies litter the streets, fields and forests. Those who are found are identified at the collection station.

Photo Document 17

Representatives of the foreign press convince themselves first-hand of the Polish atrocities committed against the ethnic Germans. Background left: Mr. Oechsner of the United Press.

Photo Document 18

Map of the major crime scenes

Location map of the major crime scenes in Poland mentioned in this book. This map dates from 1939/1940 and represents Poland as it was constituted under the Treaty of Versailles in 1919, ie. as it existed at the time of the events described in this book.

For more books on this subject and many other little-known aspects of German history, please visit us at
VersandbuchhandelScriptorium.com
and our sister site *wintersonnenwende.com* !

Featured publications include:

- the German original of "Death in Poland" by Edwin Erich Dwinger: *"Der Tod in Polen. Die volksdeutsche Passion".* Eugen Diederichs Verlag, Jena, 1940.
- *"The Polish Atrocities Against the German Minority in Poland."* Edited and published by order of the Foreign Office and based upon documentary evidence. Volk und Reich Verlag, Berlin 1940,
  as well as the German original:
- *"Die polnischen Greueltaten an den Volksdeutschen in Polen."* Im Auftrage des Auswärtigen Amtes auf Grund urkundlichen Beweismaterials zusammengestellt. Volk und Reich Verlag, Berlin 1940.

More titles are being added regularly in German and English!

www.ingramcontent.com/pod-product-compliance
Lightning Source LLC
Chambersburg PA
CBHW072159100526
44589CB00015B/2285